# SYDNEY TO SEOUL

# JOHN TORODE'S

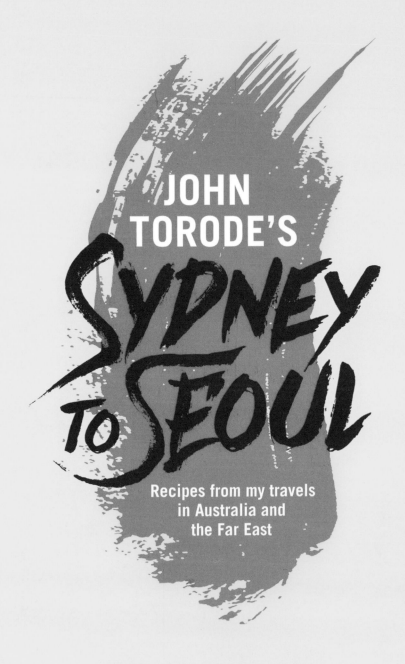

## SYDNEY TO SEOUL

Recipes from my travels
in Australia and
the Far East

Photography by Yuki Sugiura

To all the women who have taught me to cook

# CONTENTS

My love of cooking began with my Nanna, photographed here at our home in rural New South Wales with my brothers and me looking pretty smart for my first communion. Years later, I'd be cooking in Sydney harbour.

# RECIPES, TALES AND TRAVELS FROM SYDNEY TO SEOUL

This is a book of recipes collected whilst travelling the world and has been inspired by the food of every country I have visited along the way. It's a book of dreams that have come true, of recipes with tales that could be fact or fiction, but also a book full of ideas and thoughts on food and the recipes collected from streets, restaurants, friends and family.

Having been fortunate enough to travel to many a place over the past twenty years with food being the main reason, whether it be filming my own television series in Korea, Thailand and much of the rest of Asia or filming with *MasterChef*, I have seen a huge amount, met many wonderful cooks and explored lots and lots of markets and street food stalls.

Much of the food that I love has been discovered by walking. Those who know me well will tell you that I love a market, and when I say market, I mean food market. There is something about a market that allows me to soak up the culture, to hear the rhythmic chattering of the local people and the traders and to take in the all-important smells, be they pungent or intoxicating. These are the places where great food is born. Markets have long been at the centre of the community, not just somewhere to drop in and grab a bag of groceries, but a hub, a meeting place, a place to catch up with friends and mingle, and always a place to stop and eat.

Throughout my life I have been fascinated by people and how they eat, what they eat and when they eat. I love to watch people eat, using a spoon or chopsticks, fingers or hands. There is something very revealing about how people eat and there is always a story and reason why the global population have opted to all eat in different ways, using different tools and even sitting differently. How is it that through food we have all been able to keep our own national personalities? Even chopsticks can identify the origin of the food – metal, Korea, short and flat, Japan, long and rounded, China. And a fork and spoon on a table without a knife and you are in Thailand, as a knife is considered a weapon and so is never placed on the table. A huge amount of information can be gathered by looking around the streets and the street stalls anywhere in the world.

Street stalls, be they in Korea, Thailand or anywhere else in Asia, in a covered market or simply on a street corner with a few brightly coloured plastic stools and tables, are my favourite places in the world to eat.

## AN EXTRACT FROM MY DIARY AUGUST 1997

Thailand
Thursday

*Early morning market with Khun Pip (khun is a formal title and used out of respect, a bit like Mr & Mrs). Very different market to Pak Klong Talat in Bangkok – dried rats, frogs and little turtle looking things, snails as well as vegetables everywhere. Great big hydraulic coconut milk press. Khun Pip knows how to act for the cameras. Dinner last night very Thai – chicken green curry, sweet potatoes/yam and prawns, laap, tom yum, lots of chilli. Cooking lesson was slow because of cameras, really hot, laap gai, pad prik ong (surprisingly they use tomatoes). Lunch set for all of us again – red pork curry, laap, pad prik and vegetables and rice soup, as I had at breakfast.*

*Bit of filming of real river life, in a boat on the klongs. The people are really friendly and they have boats that visit each house and cook at the back doors, which are on the water, great scene, great idea. Stopped at a jetty and cooked whilst the villagers watched on as I made phat Thai. Back to the hotel and drop off King who supports Liverpool. Shoot in the Barbara Cartland suite. A busy day and loving it...*

The greatest of foods I believe are born out of necessity and came from ordinary people. They are crowd pleasers, the things that we all talk about. It could be soft corn tacos filled with pork or churros in Mexico, tteokbokki or iced noodles in Korea, wontons and soup noodles in Hong Kong, fish cakes and sweet chilli sauce or som tam in Thailand, sushi and sashimi in Japan or samosas and pani puri in India. They are always cheap, and I don't mean cheap quality, but inexpensive and delicious. These food stalls are not set up for the tourists, they are for the locals. This is where everyone goes to eat and so the food has to be good or there would be no return customers. I always gauge the deliciousness of the food in markets and street stalls by the number of people eating and waiting – the more the better. This is not food to be rushed, but savoured.

I hope that in this book and my collection of recipes you find a little inspiration and a story that maybe stays with you. It would be lovely if it gave you itchy feet and made you want to travel, not just to the most touristy of spots, but also to the markets on the outskirts of towns all over Asia, Australia and, indeed, anywhere in the world.

I know that I have been fortunate and I know also that I have been spoilt with all the destinations I have been able to visit whilst working on fantastic and exciting projects, but I have always felt honoured, always been grateful and always wanted to learn more and understand better.

Have fun with my recipes and please change what you wish. And do make dishes more spicy should you like it hot because these recipes are just a guide to the wonderful food to be enjoyed and eaten from Sydney to Seoul, and I am hoping you'll find it a helpful guide.

Best

John Torode

# STORECUPBOARD

Over the years I have been collecting all manner of sauces and condiments, some of which I still have and have only used once. So this book is not about going out and having to buy everything. The joy of a storecupboard is the slow accumulation of bits and pieces.

Shown on the photo on the next few pages are nearly all the dry goods (that means stuff that does not have to go in the fridge) to make every recipe in the book. No one is going to be buying that over a single weekend.

So I offer you a starter pack, just a few things that should be on your shelves should you decide on cooking some Asian food. These are the very basics, and I think you will be surprised at what you already have.

Everything is available online, though I do love a shop. Most big cities in the world have a Chinatown and most, if not all, things can be found there. Otherwise, get them delivered.

So start with:

a bottle of soy sauce

a tub of gochujang (Korean chilli paste)

some palm sugar

a bottle of rice vinegar

a bottle of fish sauce

and

some sesame oil

As to the rest, buy as you cook, a few things at a time. All these keep for a long time, and I mean a long time. Whilst in Korea I was given a little spoon of medicine for a swollen tummy. It was soy sauce that the monks had had in their garden for 25 years… that's a long time. Happy shopping, cooking, eating, oh, and discovering – I love that bit.

## Some notes

**Coconut milk** is used throughout this book and there are different grades, but don't worry too much as they all do the same job. Keep a tin in the fridge so that when the tin is opened, the top layer of the fatter and richer milk is set and ready to be cooked as mentioned in many of the recipes. Don't confuse coconut milk or cream with creamed coconut. Creamed coconut is a solid block of coconut milk that has been cooked and reduced and contains coconut flesh.

In this book I use **palm sugar**. It is not as sweet as our processed sugar, but is more caramelly, almost butterscotch. You can buy it in many forms, from tubs to tablets (my favourite ), blocks and even crystals. The Malaysians sometimes use a darker version from Malacca for desserts, which tastes more of coffee.

Throughout Asia the condiment of choice is **soy sauce**. It is a seasoning, as in salt, and so the richer and stronger it is, the less you need to use. Taste as you go. Once you are on your way with this book, go out and taste a few different versions – the world of soy sauce is almost as complex as beer. There are craft versions, Japanese, Thai, huge branded ones, thick and thin. The Koreans simply have two types: sauce and soup soy – guess what they use those for.

**Alcohol** is used for cooking all around the world. In Japan it's sake or rice wine and the sweeter, non-alcoholic mirin that are used for dressings and in marinades and sauces. In China it is Shaoxing rice wine, which you can substitute with sherry, and in Korea, it's soju, a sweet and strong distilled rice spirit. It works wonders in a batter because the alcohol burns off and the batter becomes super crisp. If you can't get it, use vodka.

As I have travelled and cooked I have discovered a whole host of ingredients that make a world of difference. They can be substituted, but I hope with the help of the internet you will search them out. My newest find has been **concentrated cooking tamarind**. For years I have massaged tamarind pulp with warm water to get this magical souring agent, but now I have a jar of this concentrate in the cupboard and simply use it the same way I would a stock cube, just a little bit in and taste.

Glass noodles, rice sticks, soju, Chinese (Shaoxing) rice wine, sake

Pure black pepper, sesame oil, sesame seeds, gochujang (Korean chilli paste), ssamjang (Korean spicy dipping sauce), doenjang (fermented soya bean paste), gochugaru (Korean ground chilli), apple cider vinegar, dressing soy, guk ganjang (soy sauce for soup)

Chinese rice vinegar, creamed coconut, coconut milk, ikan bilis (deep-fried crispy anchovies), belachan (shrimp paste), tamarind paste, tamarind pulp, satay sauce

Palm sugar, Thai fish sauce, shrimp paste, palm sugar, dried shrimps, oyster sauce, dried chillies, sticky rice

# BREAKFAST & BRUNCH

Breaking the fast. This is a celebration of life, of a new day. I bloody love breakfast. For me, it's a mash up of meals – breakfasty cakes that my Nanna used to make and that Sydney cafes do so well, rice and spice in Thailand and China and eggs wherever you go. Korean pickled raw octopus for breakfast? Alien or delicious? Just go for it!

# AVOCADO, CHORIZO AND SPINACH WITH CREAM DRESSING ON RYE

**SERVES 4**

50ml vegetable oil

100g chorizo, sliced

1 avocado, seed removed (see Tip)

100g young leaf spinach

freshly ground black pepper

*For the dressing*

1 egg

1 egg yolk

2 tablespoons Dijon mustard

1 tablespoon white wine vinegar

1 garlic clove, crushed

200ml vegetable oil

200ml olive oil

40g Parmesan, grated

*To serve*

4 slices of rye bread

butter, for spreading

60g Parmesan, grated

*There is something cooling about avocado and I am a sucker for a creamy dressing! This recipe typifies the Sydney to London brunch.*

In a heavy-based frying pan, heat the vegetable oil, then add the chorizo and fry over a medium heat until crisp, moving it constantly so it doesn't stick or burn. Remove from the pan and drain on kitchen paper.

Take a kitchen spoon and push it down one side of an avocado half between the flesh and the skin and run it all the way around to remove the flesh. Slice each half of flesh into four even pieces from top to bottom and set aside. Wash the spinach and set to one side in a large bowl.

Put the egg, egg yolk, mustard, vinegar and garlic into a food processor and switch it on. Blend until the mixture begins to thicken and becomes pale. Keeping the processor running, slowly pour in the oils, until smooth and combined. Thin with about 50ml hot water if the mixture seems a little thick. Stir in the Parmesan.

Add the avo slices and chorizo to the spinach and toss together, then season well with black pepper. To serve, toast the rye bread, butter it well, then place on plates and top with the avo mix. Finish with a drizzle of dressing (you probably won't need it all) and scatter over the grated Parmesan.

Tip
To remove the seed from an avocado, cut the avocado from the top until you hit the seed and then run the knife all the way down and around the seed so the avocado looks like it is cut through lengthways. Twist one half anticlockwise and the other clockwise and pull apart. The seed should be left in the centre of one half. Hold the half with the seed in one hand, then with a medium-sized sharp knife in your other hand, gently strike the seed (the knife should stick into the seed), twist the knife in an anticlockwise direction and release the seed.

# BLUEBERRY AND COCONUT PANCAKES

**MAKES ABOUT 6 GOOD-SIZED THICK PANCAKES**

350g self-raising floor

1 teaspoon bicarbonate of soda

½ teaspoon salt

1 teaspoon granulated sugar

400ml almond milk (or unsweetened coconut milk)

200ml coconut milk yoghurt (such as Co Yo)

2 eggs

100g soya spread, melted and cooled slightly (make sure it's still warm)

4 teaspoons vegetable oil, for greasing

200g blueberries

honey or maple syrup, to serve

*Thick or thin? That is usually the question, but with these beach cafe pancakes, they are thick and for good reason. There is a trick to making proper blueberry pancakes and it's got to do with when you add the blueberries. This recipe is also dairy-free for those, like me, who prefer not to have lactose, but you can substitute the non-dairy for dairy if you prefer and the recipe will work.*

In a large mixing bowl, mix together the flour, bicarb, salt and sugar. In a separate bowl, mix together the milk, yoghurt and eggs. Add the wet ingredients to the dry ones and mix together very well, then pour in the melted soy spread and give it a really good stir (the warm spread activates the bicarb so the pancakes rise). The batter should be smooth and silky but quite thick. Pour it into a large jug for easy pouring.

Warm your frying pan over a medium heat, then use a piece of kitchen paper or similar to rub a little vegetable oil around the pan, just to grease it. Now pour a good amount of the batter into the centre of the pan and let it spread out to the size of a small plate. Take a handful of the blueberries and sprinkle over the top of the pancake batter while it is still wet; the blueberries will sink in and the batter will also puff up around the outside of them.

Bubbles will start to form in the batter, so leave it to cook for a minute or so (turn your heat down if it smells like it may be cooking too quickly). When the edges are brown, the bubbles are popping and the blueberries are covered (it will look similar to the top of a crumpet), turn it over and cook for another minute or so.

Remove to a plate and keep warm while you cook the rest in the same way, making sure you keep one for yourself as they will disappear quickly! Serve with honey or maple syrup.

# APPLE AND GRANOLA CRUMBLE WITH LABNEH

**MAKES 10 SERVINGS**

*For the filling*

6 Granny Smith apples

6 Bramley apples

300g caster sugar

1 vanilla pod

100g butter

100ml apple juice

200g blackberries

*For the granola*

50ml maple syrup

60g butter

100g porridge oats

100g granola

30g dried apples

30g dried mango

30g sultanas

labneh (or natural yoghurt),
   to serve

*As a breakfast dish, I think this sums up the modern world we live in. Brunch has been big in Australia for as long as I can remember and apple crumble is a classic England pud. I am always far too full to eat apple crumble after a big roast, so why not merge the two worlds and make a breakfast that is comforting and evocative for Aussies and Poms alike? This recipe makes lots of individual breakfast pots to store in your fridge – just pull out and heat through.*

Preheat the oven to 220°C/200°C fan/gas 7.

Peel all the apples and remove the cores. Cut each apple in half, then into wedges, about eight wedges per half.

Place the apple wedges in a heavy-based pan and sprinkle the sugar over. Split the vanilla pod down the centre and scrape out as many of the seeds as possible, then add to the apples, along with the butter and apple juice. Toss the whole lot together and cover with a tight-fitting lid. Turn the heat to high and cook for 10 minutes, shuffling the pan over the heat so it all moves around and starts to cook.

Remove from the heat, add the blackberries and toss well, but be careful not to squash them. Transfer to 10 individual ovenproof dishes or ramekins and set to one side while you make the topping.

Heat the syrup and butter in a separate pan until melted and combined. Toast the oats and granola in a separate dry pan over a medium heat for about 5 minutes. Combine the melted mix, oats, granola and dried fruits and mix well.

Spoon the granola evenly over the apple and blackberry mixture in the dishes. Pop into the oven and bake for 15–20 minutes until nicely browned and crunchy on top. Serve with labneh or natural yoghurt.

# CINNAMON AND NASHI PEAR FRENCH TOAST

**SERVES 4**

2 eggs

50ml milk

1 teaspoon salt

½ baguette (preferably day-old or stale, though you can use fresh)

2 nashi (Asian) pears

60g butter

100g caster sugar

1 teaspoon ground cinnamon

squeeze of lemon juice

50ml double cream

50g Greek-style yoghurt

couple of drops of vanilla essence

finely grated zest of 1 mandarin

*French toast, eggy bread, pain perdu, whatever you wish to call it, it has been one of my favourites since my Nanna made it when I was just a little one. What I have realised over the years is that it can be given a bit of sparkle very simply. Pain perdu translates as 'lost bread', taking advantage of stale baguette, and that is what this is all about. The older bread is soaked in the egg mix while the rest of the preparation is done, and finally it is baked, which leaves you free to do something else.*

In a mixing bowl, beat the eggs with the milk and salt. Cut the baguette in half lengthways, then cut each half in half again widthways to make four pieces, so all the pieces of bread have a flat top. Add the bread pieces to the egg mix and turn to coat, then leave to soak for about 20 minutes. Meanwhile, preheat the oven to 200°C/180°C fan/gas 6.

Cut each pear into 12 equal wedges, removing the core as you go. If you are not using nashi pears, you will need to peel the pears, as nashis have a very thin skin. Melt the butter in a non-stick frying pan, then add the pear wedges and cook over a medium heat for 2 minutes. Gently stir in 50g of the sugar, the cinnamon and the squeeze of lemon juice, then remove from the heat. Leave to cool a little.

Take the soaked baguette pieces and transfer to a shallow baking tray. Spoon some of the lightly cooked pears on top of each piece, arranging six wedges on each piece and spooning over the sauce. Sprinkle with the remaining sugar, then bake in the oven for 15–20 minutes. By now the pears should have sunk into the eggy bread and the sugar and egg mix should have become crisp.

Meanwhile, mix together the cream, yoghurt, vanilla and mandarin zest, then pop it into the fridge.

Remove the baking tray from the oven and serve the French toast with the flavoured cream.

*Step-by-step pictures on pages 22–23*

# HONEY AND APPLE TEA CAKE WITH BLACKBERRY CRÈME FRAÎCHE

**MAKES 1 CAKE (SERVES MANY OR FEW, DEPENDING ON GREED!)**

*For the apple compote*

2 Granny Smith apples

1 Bramley apple

25ml runny honey

25ml maple syrup

2 teaspoons ground cinnamon

*For the cake*

250g butter, softened

250g caster sugar

½ teaspoon vanilla essence

4 eggs, beaten

300g plain flour

1 heaped teaspoon baking powder

*For the blackberry crème fraîche*

100g ripe blackberries

caster sugar, to taste (optional)

100ml crème fraîche

*My Nanna made the best apple tea cake, so this is a very personal recipe for me. The smell of it cooking takes me back to a really safe and happy time watching her cook. Miss you, Nanna!*

*When I am in Sydney there are enough cafes doing lovely breakfast-type cakes such as this one that I simply sit and drink coffee and dream of being a little boy and cooking with my greatest culinary influence.*

Preheat the oven to 180°C/160°C fan/gas 4. Grease and line a 20cm round springform tin.

Peel all the apples and remove the cores. Cut each apple into about 16 wedges, then pop them into a saucepan with the honey, syrup and 50ml water. Bring to the boil, then cook, uncovered, over a medium heat for about 10 minutes until the Grannies are soft and translucent and the Bramley has become mush. Add the cinnamon and give it a stir, then pour onto a plate and leave to cool.

In a mixing bowl, cream the butter, sugar and vanilla essence together until light and fluffy, then very slowly beat in the eggs. Fold in the flour and baking powder until combined.

Mix the apple compote into the cake mix until combined, then plonk into the prepared tin and level the surface.

Bake for 35–40 minutes until the cake is all puffed up and crispy on top. Leave to cool in the tin for 5 minutes, then turn out onto a wire rack.

To make the blackberry crème fraîche, simply squash the blackberries slightly in a bowl, then add a little sugar to sweeten, if needed. Mix in the crème fraîche. Serve the cake warm or cold with the blackberry crème fraîche.

Tip
Store any leftover cake wrapped in a tea towel and, if serving warm, heat it briefly in a microwave oven.

# HONEY RICOTTA HOT CAKES WITH APRICOT JAM

**FEEDS 4**

60g butter

pinch of salt

3 eggs

250ml buttermilk

350g plain flour

1 teaspoon baking powder

1 tablespoon runny honey

150g (drained weight) ricotta, drained

vegetable oil, for greasing

apricot jam (and/or maple syrup), to serve

*Everyone knows that Bill Granger at Bills in Sydney made these famous. He now has restaurants all around the world and you can enjoy these from London to Tokyo, but should you not have one close by, here is my revision of Bills' iconic Sydney brunch Ricotta Hot Cakes. And don't think they are just breakfast food, they also work well as a dessert and a snack for the little ones.*

Melt the butter with the salt in a small pan, then leave to cool a little. Break the eggs into a mixing bowl, add the buttermilk and whisk together well. Add the melted butter, flour, baking powder and honey and whisk together until smooth and combined. Stir in the ricotta, then leave to sit for 10 minutes.

Heat a frying pan over a medium-low heat until hot. Using a little kitchen paper, wipe the pan with a little vegetable oil. Ladle small amounts of the hot cake mix into the pan, each about the size of drop scones (you'll need to cook them in batches). The mix will puff up a bit and little bubbles will form on top as the hot cakes cook. When the cakes have light brown edges, flip them over, then cook for 2 minutes on the second side. Pile them onto a warm plate, then repeat until you have cooked all the hot cakes.

Serve the hot cakes warm with apricot jam (and/or maple syrup), or perhaps some fresh fruit or even Nutella. I like mine with a squeeze of lemon.

Try
Add some finely grated lime or lemon zest to the hot cakes batter, or a handful of chocolate chips, before cooking.

# MANGO AND GINGER BREAKFAST CAKE

**MAKES ABOUT 15 PIECES**

*For the sponge*

175g butter, softened

150g caster sugar

160g self-raising flour

½ teaspoon baking powder

1 tablespoon ground almonds

3 eggs, beaten

*For the fruit mixture*

1 small ripe mango

1 piece of stem ginger in syrup, drained and finely chopped

15g butter

15g demerara sugar

1½ tablespoons golden syrup

60g porridge oats

¼ teaspoon ground ginger

*This slab of cake (cut into smaller pieces) is a cross between a cake and a granola bar. As a cyclist, I am always on the lookout for a food bar or re-fuelling bar that I can slip in the back of my jersey to easily chew on and digest if I'm out on a big ride. Meet the newest addition to my cycling food store…*

Preheat the oven to 180°C/160°C fan/gas 4. Grease a 20 x 30cm baking (traybake) tin and line the base with a slip of greaseproof paper.

In a mixing bowl, cream the butter and caster sugar together – and I do mean cream, as in it should be twice the volume and white in colour. Now add the flour, baking powder and ground almonds and fold into the creamed mixture, slowly adding the eggs to make a basic sponge mixture. Set to one side.

Peel and remove the seed from the mango, then finely chop the flesh. Mix the mango with the stem ginger.

In a small pan, gently warm the butter, sugar and syrup together until the butter has melted. Remove from the heat and stir in the oats and ground ginger, then mix in the mango.

Fold the cake and mango mixes together, then transfer to the prepared tin, levelling the surface. Bake for 30 minutes until nicely risen and golden brown.

Cool in the tin for a minute or so, then place a plate (or board) over the tin, turn it upside down, then invert the cake onto the plate (or board), making sure all the fruit comes out too. Serve the cake warm or leave to cool completely, then cut into portions. Store any leftovers wrapped in a tea towel for up to 5 days.

# CONGEE WITH CHICKEN AND CHILLI OIL

**FEEDS 2**

1 litre strong chicken stock, plus a little extra (for the chicken)

100g minced chicken

1 skinless, boneless chicken breast, cut in half

3 tablespoons Chinese (Shaoxing) rice wine

1 thumb-sized piece of fresh root ginger, peeled and sliced

3 spring onions, halved lengthways and smashed flat with a cleaver

200g long grain rice (I use cheaper broken rice)

½ teaspoon salt

*To garnish (can include many things but classically…)*

crispy fried onions

chilli oil

whole mixed nuts and seeds

little dried fish

seaweed

bonito flakes

fresh root ginger, peeled and cut into julienne

soy sauce

good-quality sesame oil

sliced fresh red chillies, de-seeded if you like

*The breakfast choice all through Asia, but it can be a bit like Marmite, so go carefully. I like mine very seasoned, but the Chinese prefer not so much. This is my quick version, as many recipes make a stock with a whole chicken first, then the meat from the boiled chicken is used in the dish. Enjoy, and eat it more than once – I promise it will become a congee addiction.*

Put the chicken stock into a large saucepan with the minced chicken and chicken breast, the rice wine, ginger and spring onions and bring to the boil. Simmer for 5 minutes, then remove the spring onions and discard. Take out the chicken breast and set to one side on a plate. You are now left with the stock to cook the rice in.

Add the rice to the stock, then bring to the boil and stir. Reduce the heat to low, cover with a lid, then simmer for about 1½ hours, until the congee is the consistency of thin porridge, stirring frequently during the last 30 minutes of the cooking time. Congee will continue to thicken as it stands (so you can thin it with a little water or more stock, if need be).

Season the congee with the salt. Heat the chicken breast in a little extra stock for about 2 minutes until hot, then shred it and place on top on the congee, along with the crispy fried onions and a little chilli oil. Serve with all the remaining garnishes in little bowls alongside.

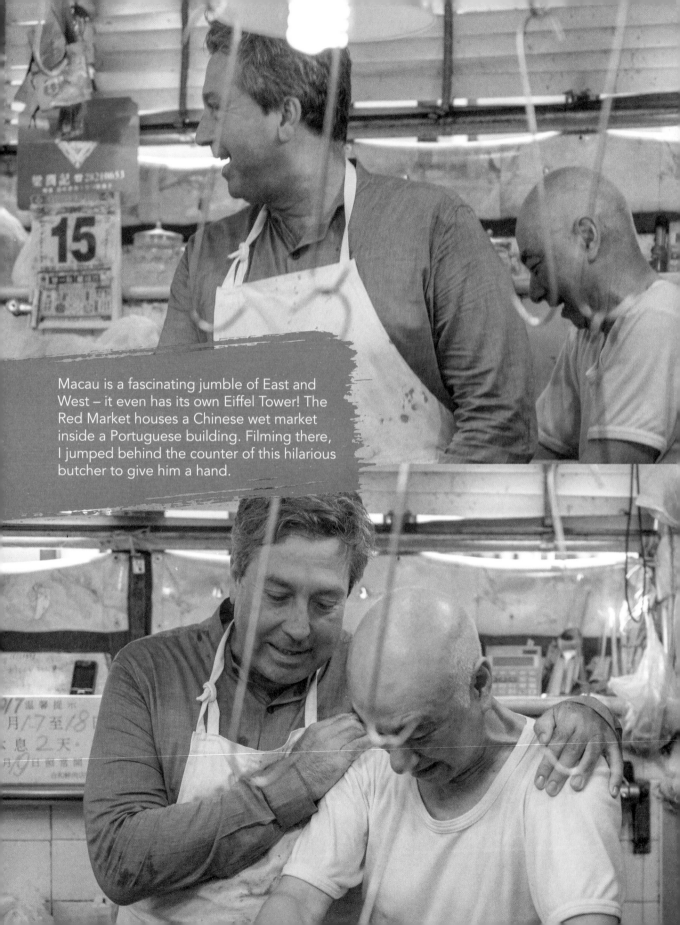

Macau is a fascinating jumble of East and West – it even has its own Eiffel Tower! The Red Market houses a Chinese wet market inside a Portuguese building. Filming there, I jumped behind the counter of this hilarious butcher to give him a hand.

# SPICY EGGS

. . . . . . . . . . . . . . . . . . . . . . . . . . . . . . . . . . . . . . . . . . . . . . . . . . .

**FOR 2**

100ml olive oil

20 cherry tomatoes, cut in half

2 small fresh red chillies,
    finely sliced

1 garlic clove, crushed

200ml vegetable oil, for
    deep-frying

4 eggs

freshly ground black pepper

rice, to serve (optional)

*These little deep-fried, crispy eggs with a spicy tomato sauce remind me
of many an early morning searching out a roadside breakfast when I'm
travelling. Spice and eggs can be a bit tricky, but the addition of a sweet
tomato sauce makes for a hearty breakfast or anytime-of-the-day snack.*

. . . . . . . . . . . . . . . . . . . . . . . . . . . . . . . . . . . . . . . . . . . . . . . . . . .

Take a heavy-based pan, pour in the olive oil, then lay the tomatoes, cut
side down, in the pan. Cook over a medium heat for 2 minutes, then
sprinkle in the chilli slices and garlic, turn the tomatoes over and season
with black pepper. Cook for a further 2 minutes, then remove from the
heat and leave to one side.

Pour the vegetable oil into a deep frying pan or wok and heat to 180°C.
Break an egg into a cup, then slide the egg into the hot oil; repeat with
the remaining eggs. Deep-fry until the eggs are crispy around the edges
and blistered all over, about 2 minutes.

Using a slotted spoon, lift the eggs from the oil and drain well on kitchen
paper, then drop them on top of the tomato mix. Serve with cooked
rice, if you like.

*Step-by-step pictures on pages 36–37*

Deep-frying eggs is as quick as a wink and in real terms they're just poached eggs, but poached in oil. When the oil is shimmering, slide in the eggs and deep-fry for about 2 minutes until the eggs go crispy and bubble up, but the yolks are still runny (unless you prefer to cook them a bit more).

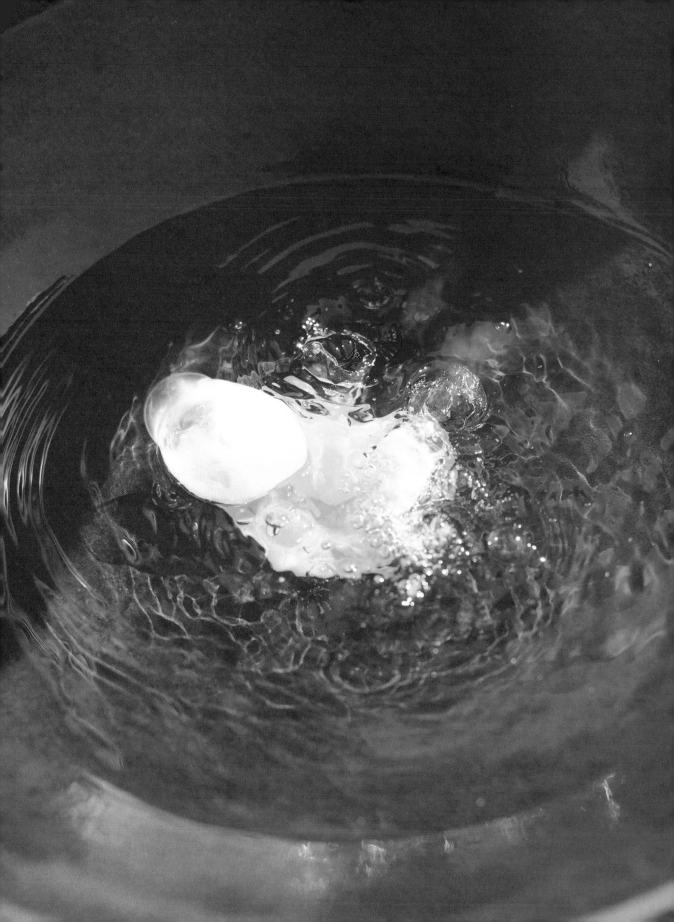

# AUSSIE-STYLE GRAINS BOWL

............................................................

**FEEDS AT LEAST 2**

4 different cooked (cold) grains
    and ½ cup (about
    3 tablespoons) of each
    (see Tip)

2 spring onions, finely sliced

2 handfuls of fresh flat-leaf
    parsley, chopped

*For the dressing*

2 teaspoons tahini

2 teaspoons olive oil

2 teaspoons apple
    cider vinegar

4 teaspoons fresh lime juice

1 long fresh red chilli,
    finely diced

small thumb-sized piece of
    fresh root ginger, peeled and
    very finely diced

*For the topping*

1 cooked chicken breast, sliced

1 avocado, sliced, with lemon
    juice squeezed over

2 soft-boiled eggs, peeled and
    each cut in half (optional)

a handful of beansprouts

salt

*This is simply a full-on protein brunch with a few carbs added for good measure. As for the grains you use, do as the Australians do and mix them up, playing around with different combinations. Sometimes I eat it cold and sometimes I eat it hot; sometimes with sprouted beans and sometimes without, but I do like the chicken and avo combo.*

............................................................

In a serving bowl, mix the cooked grains with the spring onions and chopped parsley.

Make the dressing by mixing together the tahini, olive oil, vinegar, lime juice, chilli and ginger in a small bowl. Season to taste with a little salt.

Drizzle a little dressing over the mixed grains and toss gently to mix. Top with the chicken, avo and eggs (if using), then drizzle over some more dressing. Finish with the beansprouts. This is the best it is going to look, so it's time to get stuck in.

Tip
There are plenty of new and exciting grains coming on the market, but grains that are good for this dish include quinoa, black quinoa, red rice, brown and wild rice, green lentils, pearl barley, bulgur, chickpeas, farro, round barley, pinhead oatmeal, buckwheat, spelt and whole rye. Simply cook them according to the packet instructions, then cool quickly and store in a tightly covered container in the fridge.

# HONG KONG MACARONI SOUP

**ENOUGH FOR 2**

100g macaroni

500ml chicken stock or broth

2 eggs

a little vegetable oil

100g smoked ham, chopped

freshly ground black pepper,
   to taste

*The last time I went to Hong Kong I was taken to The Hong Kong Tea Restaurant. Tea restaurants are known as* cha chaan teng, *and I ate this for my breakfast – all I wanted after that was to go back every day. I had char siu, or Chinese BBQ pork, in mine, but I have used smoked ham in this recipe. However, do try it with BBQ pork if you can get it, it's ace.*

Cook the macaroni according to the packet directions.

Bring the chicken stock to the boil, drop in the cooked macaroni and bring back to the boil.

Meanwhile, fry the eggs in a little oil.

Spoon out the soup into two bowls, drop the ham on top and add the fried eggs. Grind over a little pepper to serve.

Brekkie – Honkers style.

# STREET FOOD

Street food is the real reason I fell in love with Asian cooking. Stumbling across a stall in Bangkok on an early visit, I found the most wonderful culinary sight. A cauldron filled with boiling oil and a Thai lady scooping in handfuls of paste, while a man with a stick moved the oil slowly so the paste became part of an oil vortex. To his side a girl plucked out the now fried and fragrant fish cakes into little plastic bags. Each bag was attached to two others of diced cucumber and crushed peanuts and chilli sauce, tied by red rubber bands and looking just like those bags you used to bring goldfish home in. That day I stood and watched, learnt and smelt and felt alive.

# THAI FISH CAKES

........................................................

**SERVES 4–6**

*For the fish cakes*

100g skinless salmon fillet

100g skinless cod fillet

150g prepared squid (or cuttlefish)

30g red curry paste (bought or see page 138)

8 lime leaves, very finely shredded (see Tip)

2 snake (yard long) beans, chopped

1 tablespoon fish sauce

1 large egg white

1 tablespoon oyster sauce

200ml vegetable oil, for deep-frying

*To serve*

a handful of fresh coriander sprigs

sweet chilli sauce (see page 47 or buy a bottle)

2 fresh red chillies, de-seeded and finely diced

½ cucumber, de-seeded and diced

15g roasted peanuts, chopped

*This is one of the easiest Thai snacks, but it is also one of the most misunderstood. The texture of the fish cakes should be slightly rubbery, with a textured outer coating. They should contain a good amount of spice and lots of lime leaves. I have done my utmost to be as authentic as I can with this recipe.*

........................................................

Blend the salmon, cod and squid in a food processor until smooth. Add the red curry paste and pulse until well mixed.

Put all the other ingredients, except the vegetable oil, in a bowl. Mix in the fish mixture, then knead everything together for 5 minutes until smooth and elastic. To achieve a texture similar to the fish cakes from Thai street stalls, you should literally throw the paste into the bowl several times to make the mixture more elastic.

Heat the vegetable oil in a wok or deep frying pan to 180°C or until the oil bubbles up around the handle of a wooden spoon. Drop heaped teaspoonfuls of the mixture into the hot oil and deep-fry the fish cakes in batches over a medium heat until golden, about 4 minutes. Drain on kitchen paper.

Serve the fish cakes with a scattering of fresh coriander and a bowl of the sweet chilli sauce mixed with the chilli and cucumber and the chopped peanuts on top.

Tip
Lime leaves are actually 'double' leaves in the shape of an hourglass, so here I am using 8 lime leaves, so 16 singles.

*Step-by-step pictures on page 46*

# SWEET CHILLI SAUCE

......................................................

**MAKES 1 SMALL BOTTLE**

1 red pepper, de-seeded and chopped

4 long fresh red chillies, cut in half and de-seeded

150g caster sugar

150ml white wine vinegar or Chinese rice vinegar

*You can buy this if you like, but this is my quick recipe. It keeps for a few weeks in the fridge. It's a great storecupboard staple.*

......................................................

Place all the ingredients in a medium saucepan with 100ml water and bring to the boil over a high heat. Reduce to a simmer and cook for about 10 minutes until it turns pinkish.

Remove from the heat and leave to cool slightly, then transfer to a food processor and blend until smooth.

Return to the pot and cook, stirring occasionally, until slightly sticky, about 10 minutes.

Cool again, then serve or store in a sealed bottle or jar in the fridge and use as required.

# TOFU AGEDASHI

. . . . . . . . . . . . . . . . . . . . . . . . . . . . . . . . . .

**FOR 4 AS A STARTER**

200ml vegetable oil, for
    deep-frying

300g firm tofu

1 tablespoon rice flour
    (or cornflour)

pinch of salt

2 packets of miso soup mix

2 spring onions, finely
    chopped, to sprinkle

bonito flakes, to sprinkle

soy sauce, to serve

*My love of food has always taken me on a fantastic journey and now my
girlfriend's food has inspired and intrigued me with its different style. This
is light, pretty and very, very delicious. Not an absolute classic, I admit, as
I have played with the recipe to make it quicker and easier. If you want to
make a vegetarian version, use a veg miso soup mix and omit the bonito.*

. . . . . . . . . . . . . . . . . . . . . . . . . . . . . . . . . . . . . . . . . . . . . .

Heat the vegetable oil in a deep frying pan or wok to 180°C.

Cut the tofu into 12 equal-sized squares. Mix the rice flour with the salt
and roll the tofu pieces in it to coat all over.

Drop a few pieces of tofu at a time into the hot oil and deep-fry for
3 minutes, or until they float and the outside is golden. Remove and
drain. Repeat with the rest of the tofu pieces, allowing the oil to come
back up to temperature after each batch, until they are all cooked
and drained.

Meanwhile, mix the miso soup according to the packet instructions, then
heat it as instructed. Pour 100ml of the hot soup into four little bowls.
Take the tofu and pop three pieces into each bowl so it sits up out of
the soup.

Sprinkle with the spring onions and bonito and serve with a little soy
on the side.

# BINDAETTOEK (MUNG BEAN PANCAKES)

**MAKES 2 BIG ONES (OR LOTS OF SMALL ONES) – GREAT AS A PARTY NIBBLE**

100g dried split yellow mung beans (mung dhal)

¾ teaspoon salt

2 tablespoons kimchi juice (from the jar or packet)

100g kimchi, finely chopped

100g beansprouts

2 spring onions, chopped

2 teaspoons good-quality sesame oil

½ teaspoon minced garlic

¼ teaspoon freshly ground black pepper

2 teaspoons gochugaru (Korean ground chilli)

100ml vegetable oil, for frying

1 fresh green chilli, finely sliced, to garnish

rice vinegar, to serve

slices of red onion, to serve

*Before travelling to Korea, I had never eaten Bindaettoek and I'm not sure why. I was introduced to them when they were being made in a market in Seoul and I sat and watched the beans being pounded with water to make a paste and fried in front of me. They were so good that after filming and when we finished late, a few of us would wander to a little local place and eat these, sometimes plain, sometimes with minced pork, but always hot and always crispy on the edges, which for me is the best bit. You can now buy kimchi in a jar or packet from many supermarkets, but if you want to make your own, there is a quick recipe on page 244.*

Start by making the batter. Soak the dried mung beans in enough cold water to cover for at least 3 hours (or overnight) to soften.

Once soaked, drain the mung beans and then tip them into a food processor along with 100ml fresh water. Add the salt and blitz to create a smooth paste – it'll still be stickier than a regular batter, but if the food processor stops, add a little more water to loosen, along with the kimchi juice. Pour into a mixing bowl and stir in the kimchi, beansprouts, spring onions, sesame oil, garlic, black pepper and gochugaru.

Pour half the vegetable oil into a frying pan and heat over a high heat. Spoon half the batter into the hot oil and spread evenly, then cook for a couple of minutes until the edges start to colour – spin it around in the pan so you know it's cooked; if it sticks it's not ready. You will have to regulate your heat here, so you get it golden brown and don't burn it.

Flip the pancake once it's crispy on the underside and then press in a few slices of green chilli (for heat and garnish) on the second side. Fry for a further 2 or so minutes until it's cooked through and golden, then remove and drain on kitchen paper.

Repeat with the remaining oil and batter to make two big pancakes. Mix together the vinegar and sliced onions to dip the pancakes into.

# SOM TAM (GREEN PAPAYA SALAD)

**ENOUGH FOR 4**

500g unripe green papaya or green mango (300g flesh), peeled and thinly sliced into julienne

5 fresh red or green bird's eye chillies, sliced

3 garlic cloves, peeled

1 tablespoon dried shrimps, soaked (see Tip on page 154)

2 tablespoons unsalted roasted peanuts

50g snake (yard long) beans, cut into 1cm lengths

1 tablespoon palm sugar

6 cherry tomatoes, quartered (optional)

1 tablespoon fish sauce

3 tablespoons lime juice

*This may be a salad, but it is also the greatest and most wonderful street food of Thailand. Although it originated in Isaan, or northeast Thailand, it is served all over the country. It is always made to order and pounded in front of you with a few extras like salty crab, if you wish. It should be salty, sweet, sour and hot... oh yeah, hot. Not just pet pet but pet ma as they say. Pet means 'hot' and ma means 'oh ma!'*

Take a quarter of the papaya and all the chillies and garlic and pound using a mortar and pestle until you nearly have a paste. Add the dried shrimps, peanuts and snake beans and pound a little to break them up.

Add the rest of the papaya and the palm sugar and tomatoes, if using, and pound together. Now add the fish sauce and lime juice and pound some more.

I prefer to eat mine standing on a street corner in Bangkok, but, at home, scoop onto a plate, eat and be transported to the street food capital of the world.

*Step-by-step pictures on pages 52–53*

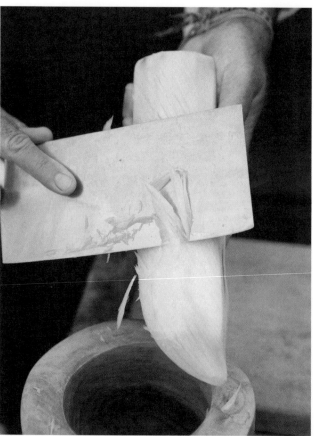

# AVOCADO AND PRAWN TEMPURA

**SERVES 6**

700ml vegetable oil, for deep-frying

60ml soda water, chilled

120g cornflour, plus 20g to coat the prawns and avocado

pinch of salt

2 ice cubes

2 avocados, halved

12 large fresh raw prawns, peeled but leave the heads and tails on

juice of 2 lemons

*For the dipping sauce*

soy sauce

1 fresh red chilli, sliced

*Not classic street food, but more one of those New World food vans or market stalls found from Korea to Sydney. Taking two of the very best things to put into tempura batter and serving them quickly and hot – perfect. Make sure the oil is hot so the batter becomes nice and crisp. If you want to make a purely vegetarian version, use mushrooms and tofu.*

Pour the vegetable oil into a wok or deep-fat fryer and heat to 180°C. The oil will start to shimmer when ready. In a mixing bowl, mix the chilled soda water with the 120g cornflour and salt and whisk to a smooth paste. Drop the ice cubes into the mixture to keep it cool.

Peel and slice each half of the avocado into six pieces. Place the avocado and prawns on two separate plates and squeeze the lemon juice over both.

When the oil is hot, stir the batter well, dust the prawns with the remaining cornflour and then dip them into the batter.

One at a time, drop the battered prawns into the oil but do this in two batches so the oil stays hot. Give the oil time to come back up to temperature after the first batch is taken out, and turn up the heat if need be to keep the prawns frying. When they float to the top, cook for a further minute, then remove and drain on kitchen paper. Deep-fry the remaining prawns and drain as before.

Repeat the same process of dusting, battering and deep-frying with the avocado slices.

Stack the crisp battered prawns and avocado slices on little plates and serve with the soy sauce mixed with the sliced chilli.

Tip
When deep-frying, never leave the pan unattended, ensure that the handle is not protruding from the stove, and have a tight-fitting lid to hand to cover the pan quickly if the oil should ignite (though this is very unlikely if you are careful!).

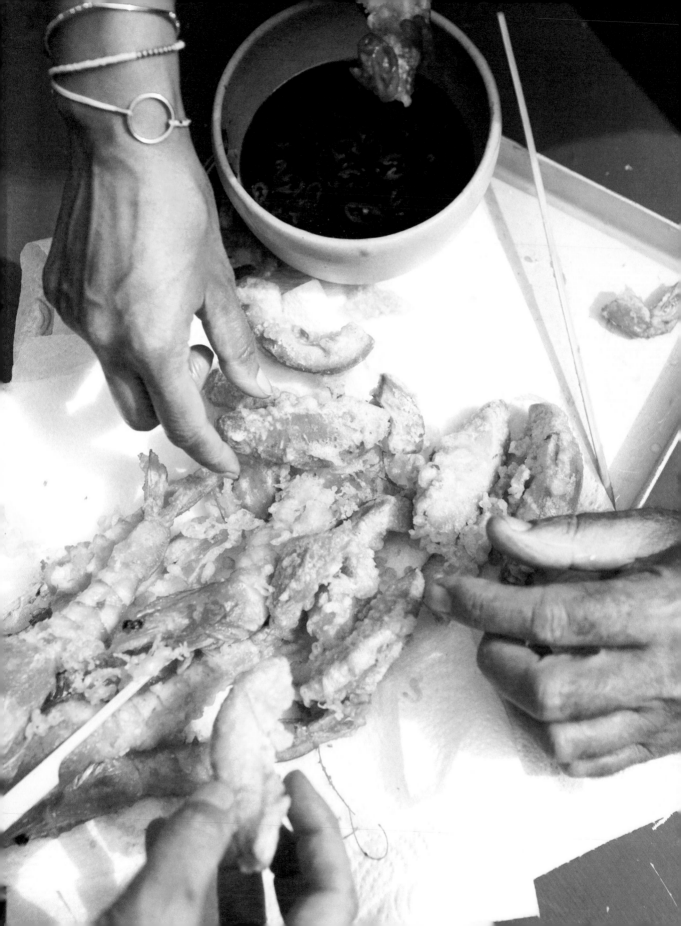

# PORK AND BEAN CURD ROLLS

**MAKES 8 ROLLS**

100g pork fat, cut into long
   thin strips

1 tablespoon sugar

1 tablespoon light soy sauce

1 tablespoon dark soy sauce

3 heaped tablespoons
   potato flour

1 tablespoon freshly ground
   black pepper

1 tablespoon salt

1 tablespoon Chinese
   five-spice powder

450g pork fillets, gristle
   removed, cut into long,
   thin strips

1 spring onion, finely diced

8 water chestnuts, cut into
   thin strips

3 garlic cloves, pounded
   until fine

2 dried bean curd sheets (tau
   peoy), cut into 8 rectangles,
   each about 18cm wide

peanut or vegetable oil,
   for deep-frying

1 cucumber, sliced, for serving

*For the dipping sauce*

4 tablespoons chilli sauce

1 tablespoon sugar

1 tablespoon lime juice

1 garlic clove, pounded
   until fine

½ teaspoon salt

1–2 tablespoons toasted
   sesame seeds

*Some of you will by now have noticed that many of my recipes have been taught to me by people in their own homes. This recipe for Ngoh Hiang or Lor Bak is from a very glamorous Chinese Malaysian lady, called Pearly Kee.*

*Whilst cooking in her outside kitchen, I tapped my spoon on the side of a metal bowl and she properly told me off for making too much noise. She told me that her neighbours did not need to know she was cooking and to be quiet. I have listened to that bit of advice and now make a lot less noise in the kitchen!*

Blanch the pork fat in hot water for 3–4 minutes to soften, then drain and leave to cool.

In a big mixing bowl, mix together all the seasonings (sugar, soy sauces, potato flour, pepper, salt and five-spice powder) with 2 tablespoons of water – the mixture should be sticky and not runny.

Add the pork and blanched pork fat and mix thoroughly. Leave to rest for 15 minutes before wrapping (you can leave it to season overnight in the fridge at this stage, if you prefer – just cover the bowl and refrigerate).

Once you are ready to wrap, add the spring onion, water chestnuts and garlic to the pork mixture, adding a few more tablespoons of water if the mixture is dry.

For each roll, top a bean curd rectangle with three scoops of the marinated meat mixture, spreading it evenly and keeping the mixture about 1cm away from both ends. Starting from the long end, roll up gently to enclose the filling, then cut off the bean curd sheet with a knife where the overlap meets – avoid a large overlap as the double layer will cause the meat to cook unevenly. The moisture of the sheet will seal the two ends naturally. Repeat with the remaining bean curd rectangles until all the marinated meat is used up.

# PORK AND BEAN CURD ROLLS

(continued)

Pour enough vegetable oil into a wok or heavy-based saucepan to reach a depth of 5cm and heat until it reaches 180°C. The oil will start to shimmer when ready.

Add three or four rolls to the hot oil, then turn these over after 3 minutes or so and cook the other side. The rolls are cooked when the sizzling stops. Remove the rolls to some kitchen paper and leave to drain. Deep-fry the remaining rolls in the same way, allowing the oil to come back up to temperature after each batch, until they are all cooked and drained. Leave to cool.

For the dipping sauce, in a small bowl, simply mix all the ingredients together, except the sesame seeds, until the sugar dissolves, then check the flavour and adjust accordingly. Just before serving, sprinkle on the toasted sesame seeds.

Once the rolls are cool, cut each roll into six bite-sized pieces and serve with the dipping sauce and cucumber slices.

新記
家記 鮮肉
家禽
食品
超

新記
Sun

Tel:
2854 1800

My first stop anywhere in the world is
a market – even if I have to catch a ferry
to it! This one is on Hong Kong island
and is well worth the journey.

# POH PIA (THAI PORK AND PRAWN SPRING ROLLS)

. . . . . . . . . . . . . . . . . . . . . . . . . . . . . . . . . . . . . . . . . .

**MAKES ABOUT 20**

100g dried rice vermicelli

2–3 garlic cloves, peeled

a bunch of fresh coriander,
   separated into stems
   and leaves

2 teaspoons white peppercorns

pinch of salt

1.5 litres vegetable oil,
   for deep-frying

250g peeled and deveined raw
   tiger prawns, minced

500g minced pork

2 tablespoons fish sauce

50g palm sugar

50g beansprouts

100g small Thai shallots,
   chopped

50g plain flour

a packet of spring roll wrappers
   (about 20)

sweet chilli sauce (see
   page 47 or buy a bottle)

*It's funny how trends come and go. Spring rolls were all the rage ten years ago, and now trying to find good ones is really difficult. For me they must be stuffed full of goodies, which means spending a bit of time making them.*

. . . . . . . . . . . . . . . . . . . . . . . . . . . . . . . . . . . . . . . . . .

Soak the noodles in warm water for about 30 minutes, then drain.

Using a mortar and pestle, pound together the garlic, coriander stems, peppercorns and a pinch of salt until a fine paste forms.

Heat 2 tablespoons of the oil in a wok over a medium heat and fry the garlic/coriander paste until fragrant, about 3 minutes, stirring all the time. Add the prawns and pork and stir-fry for 3 minutes until cooked. Pour over the noodles and leave so the noodles take up all the liquid from the cooked prawns and pork, then stir and season with the fish sauce and palm sugar.

Tip the mixture into a heatproof bowl and leave to cool. Use a pair of scissors to cut up the noodles a little, then mix in the beansprouts, coriander leaves and shallots.

In a bowl, mix the flour with a little water to make a paste. Lay the wrappers on a worktop, a few at a time, with a corner of each facing towards you, and place a good tablespoonful of filling in the centre of each one. Roll up from the corner and then fold over the left and right sides. Roll each wrapper until it has almost reached the top and seal with the paste. Repeat with the remaining wrappers and filling. You don't have to cook the rolls immediately, but don't wrap in clingfilm or they sweat and can be soggy and explode on cooking. Cook the same day.

Set the rolls aside for 1 hour to allow the paste to dry and seal the rolls. At this stage, you can also transfer them to a tray or plate (in a single layer) and refrigerate them to cook later the same day.

Pour the remaining oil into a wok or large heavy-based saucepan and heat over a medium heat until it reaches 180°C. The oil will start to shimmer when ready.

Place four or five spring rolls at a time in the hot oil and deep-fry for about 5 minutes, or until crispy and golden all over, turning occasionally. Remove and drain on kitchen paper. Repeat with the remaining spring rolls, allowing the oil to come back up to temperature after each batch, until they are all cooked and drained. Serve with sweet chilli sauce.

*Step-by-step pictures on pages 62–63*

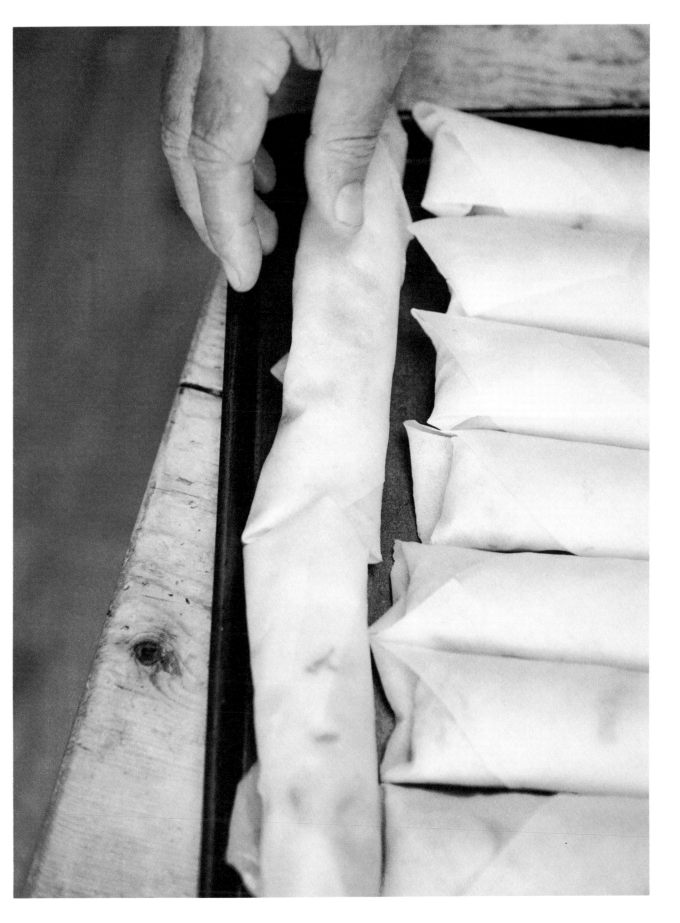

# MA HOR (GALLOPING HORSES)

**FEEDS A CROWD**

vegetable oil, for frying and deep-frying

500g minced chicken

500g minced pork

500g minced fresh raw prawns

10 garlic cloves, peeled

4 fresh coriander roots, soaked and washed (see Tip)

2 teaspoons white peppercorns

pinch of salt

100g palm sugar

75ml fish sauce

2 tablespoons crispy fried onions

30g roasted peanuts, crushed

*To serve*

1 large pineapple, peeled, quartered, cored and cut into wedges

3 large fresh red chillies, de-seeded and cut into julienne

fresh coriander leaves

*'Galloping horses' – there is always a story about Thai food, and this one is said to come from a royal court when they needed a small nibble to serve but had no time to cook. Or maybe it was the hungry hordes that arrived on galloping horses. You will notice that white pepper is the spice and the chilli is only a garnish; some say this is because it was a recipe invented before the chilli arrived in Asia and instead peppercorns were used for spice.*

Heat a little vegetable oil in a frying pan, add the minced chicken and fry until cooked through. Transfer to a plate lined with kitchen paper to drain. Repeat with the pork and prawns, cooking them separately. Leave to cool, then mix them together.

Using a mortar and pestle, pound the whole garlic cloves, the coriander roots and white peppercorns with some salt until fine.

Heat some more vegetable oil in a wok, add the garlic/coriander paste and fry gently until fragrant, about 3 minutes, stirring all the time. Add the palm sugar and fish sauce and heat to dissolve the sugar and make it sticky. Add the combined minced meat and prawns, then simmer for 5 minutes until the mixture comes together and is bound. Check the flavour and adjust with a little more salt, if necessary. Remove the mixture from the heat and leave to cool.

Mix the crispy fried onions with the crushed peanuts, then add to the minced meat and prawns mix and stir together.

Cut the pineapple slices into smaller wedges. Place the fruit on a serving platter, then top with spoonfuls of the minced meat and prawns mix and garnish with the chillies and coriander leaves.

Tip
To prep coriander root, I soak and wash fresh roots to get the dirt off (soaking them first makes them easier to clean), then drain. There's no need to peel them, though.

# BOSSAM (GLAZED PORK BELLY AND STICKY SAUCE)

**SERVES 6–8**

1.5kg boneless pork belly (skin on)

1 spring onion

1 onion, peeled

10 garlic cloves, peeled

1 bay leaf, lightly crushed

125g fresh root ginger, peeled

1 tablespoon black peppercorns

lettuce leaves, to serve

*For the marinade*

2 tablespoons doenjang (fermented soy bean paste)

5 tablespoons Korean rice wine or mirin

*For the glaze*

1 tablespoon doenjang (fermented soya bean paste)

4–5 tablespoons Korean rice syrup

200ml soy sauce

200ml Korean rice wine

1 fresh chilli, sliced in half

50g hunk of fresh root ginger

2 garlic cloves, peeled and roughly bashed

*I am a real pork belly lover and this recipe now sits at about number three in my favourites, only beaten by my five-hour pork belly and Chinese crispy roast pork – this really is ace.*

*Having spent a day with a wise old lady in the Korean countryside learning how soy sauce is made and inspecting her two thousand odd pots full of different jangs, or pastes and sauces (see pages 246–247), I was treated to this dish, my first taste of Bossam.*

Mix the marinade ingredients together. Coat the pork belly in the marinade and leave to marinate, ideally overnight.

The next day, put the spring onion, onion, garlic cloves, bay leaf, ginger and peppercorns into a large saucepan.

Add the pork belly and enough water to just cover the meat. Bring to the boil, then reduce to a low heat and put a lid on the pan. Simmer, well not really simmer, more let it tick over, for 2–3 hours. Once cooked through and tender, gently lift the pork out of the pan and leave to one side, skin-side up, so that the skin dries and firms up slightly.

Meanwhile, put all the glaze ingredients into a saucepan, place over a medium heat and bring to the boil. Turn down, allowing the sauce to simmer until reduced by about a third and to become glossy and caramel-like.

Remove the chilli, ginger and garlic from the glaze, pour over the pork and leave to sit and cool a little before cutting into slabs of deliciousness. Serve with lettuce leaves to wrap up the pork.

# CURRY PUFFS

............................................

**MAKES ABOUT 24**

*For the water pastry*

300g plain flour

½ teaspoon salt

125ml lukewarm water

1 small egg, beaten

1 tablespoon vegetable oil

*For the grease dough*

150g plain flour, plus extra
for dusting

75g cold butter, diced

*For the filling*

4 teaspoons vegetable oil

1 large onion, diced

2 tablespoons Malaysian
curry powder

100g cooked cold
potatoes, diced

50g frozen peas

200g cooked cold chicken,
shredded

100ml thick curry sauce mix
(you can buy this, look for
brands such as Golden Curry)

salt

a little milk, for glazing (if using
puff pastry)

*Karipap Pusing (curry puffs) are a street treat found all over Malaysia, and
the influence of all the different cultures is wrapped in these little parcels
– a bit of Indian curry, some Chinese, Malay and even Portuguese with
the pastry (the same pastry is used in Portuguese custard tarts). If you
don't want to make the pastry, use 500g ready-rolled puff pastry.*

............................................

Mix all the ingredients for the water pastry together in a bowl to form a
soft dough, then divide into two balls and set to one side to cool.

Meanwhile, make the grease dough. Put the flour into a bowl and add
the butter. Using a table knife and a fork, cut the butter into the flour
until it resembles crumbly, coarse sand. Knead by hand until it turns shiny
and smooth and is dough-like in consistency. This process takes a while,
so get ready for a work-out! Divide into two balls and set to one side.

Heat the oil in a saucepan, add the onion and cook until soft. Stir in the
curry powder and cook for 3 minutes until fragrant. Add the potatoes,
peas and chicken, coat with the spice mix, then season with salt. Add the
curry sauce and 50ml water and mix so the sauce coats everything and
the filling is heated through. Set aside to cool completely.

Wrap one ball of the water dough around one ball of the greased dough
to enclose it completely. The water dough is very pliable so this will be
easy to do. On a lightly floured surface, roll the combined dough into a
thin oval shape. Roll it up and with one end facing you, roll the dough
out again into an oval. Roll the dough up and out again as before, then
slice across into 1cm discs. Flatten each disc with the palm of your hand
and spirals will be visible. Be gentle as the dough easily splits into layers.

If using puff pastry, starting from a long edge, roll up, then cut across
into 1cm slices as above and brush the rounds with a little milk.

Put a dessertspoon of the curry filling into the centre of each flattened
disc and fold over. Seal the edges together by pinching and folding the
dough edges to form a rope (if you have a curry puff mould, use it!). Line
the puffs up on a greased baking sheet like soldiers, brushing with milk if
you've used puff. Transfer to the fridge and they can sit there for up to a
day, or you can cook them later, but they need to be cool before baking.

Preheat the oven to 200°C/180°C fan/gas 6. Bake the puffs for about
25–30 minutes or until crisp and golden. Serve them warm. Yum!

Tip
This is one of the best ways to use up leftover cooked chicken.

............................................

# MANDU (KOREAN DUMPLINGS)

**MAKES 22**

22 mandu/gyoza skins

vegetable oil, for frying

*For the filling*

25g sweet potato noodles
    (dangmyeon)

150g kimchi, minced and
    drained (bought or see
    page 244)

150g minced pork

75g firm tofu

½ spring onion, finely chopped

½ teaspoon minced garlic

½ teaspoon minced fresh
    root ginger

1 egg

1½ teaspoons gochugaru
    (Korean ground chilli)

1 teaspoon soy sauce

1 tablespoon good-quality
    sesame oil

1 teaspoon mirin

salt and freshly ground
    black pepper

*For the dipping sauce*

4 tablespoons soy sauce

4 tablespoons rice vinegar

2 spring onions, finely chopped

¼ fresh red chilli, finely
    chopped

¼ teaspoon minced garlic

*Eat these in broth or just as they are. On one outing I even went to a factory where they made mandu. Everything was fresh and from the local community. They make three million mandu EVERY DAY, yep, every day!*

*It seems that every culture has its own dumpling, be it eastern Europe with its pelmeni, Italy and its ravioli, Japan and its gyoza, or Korea and its mandu. When I first saw these I thought they were tortelloni, as they are a similar shape, though they are made slightly differently and the flavour is definitely of Korea – including kimchi, sesame and spring onions.*

Soak the sweet potato noodles in boiling water for 5 minutes to soften, then drain and chop.

Put the kimchi, minced pork, tofu and all the other ingredients for the filling into a bowl, along with the chopped noodles, and mix together well, seasoning with salt and pepper.

Put a spoonful of the filling in the middle of each mandu skin, then wet the edges with water, fold over and press together to form semi-circles.

Take each semi-circular mandu, fold over and pinch the two corners together to seal to make the mandu look like large tortelloni.

You can either fry or steam the mandu:

**Fried mandu**
Brush a cold frying pan (with a lid) with vegetable oil, then place the mandu in the cold pan in a Catherine wheel formation. Put the pan over a medium heat (this is the frying bit), then leave to colour for 2 minutes or until the bottoms of the mandu are light brown.

Pour in 100ml water, then cover the pan and leave to steam for about 2 minutes. Remove the lid and cook until all the water has evaporated and they start to fry and sizzle again.

**Steamed mandu**
Place in a steamer, in batches if necessary, over a pan of boiling water and cook until they are soft and the wrappers become translucent, about 12 minutes.

Put the soy sauce and vinegar into a small serving bowl, along with the spring onions, chilli and garlic. Mix well.

Arrange the hot mandu on a plate and serve with the bowl of dipping sauce alongside.

# CRAB, CHICKEN AND GLASS NOODLE SALAD

**ENOUGH FOR 8 PEOPLE**

*For the salad*
200g glass noodles (mung
  bean thread or cellophane
  noodles)
a handful of fresh Vietnamese
  mint, leaves picked
a handful of fresh regular mint,
  leaves picked
a handful of fresh coriander,
  leaves picked
a handful of fresh Thai basil,
  leaves picked
10 pak chee laos leaves (or you
  can use extra coriander)
1 cucumber, de-seeded and cut
  into half-moons

*For the dressing (nam jim)*
juice of 3 limes
2 garlic cloves, peeled
5 small Thai shallots, halved
3 long fresh red chillies
40g palm sugar
40ml fish sauce
3 fresh coriander roots, soaked
  and washed

*For the chicken and
  crab combo*
200g finely minced chicken
2 teaspoons roasted chilli
  powder (see Tip)
2 small Thai shallots, sliced
100g picked fresh white
  crabmeat
1 fresh red or fresh green
  chilli, julienned
a handful of fresh
  coriander leaves

50g roast rice (see Tip on
  page 81), ground, to serve

*Once upon a time I was wandering around a market in Bangkok and was tempted by this little salad. It was amazing! It was not just the clash of massive flavours, the tingling of my lips from the lime and chilli or the texture of the noodles, what appealed most was how this way-out-there combination of ingredients worked so beautifully.*

Soak the glass noodles in boiling water for 2 minutes until hydrated, then drain.

To make the dressing, using a mortar and pestle, pound together the lime juice, garlic, shallots, chillies, palm sugar, fish sauce and coriander roots until smooth and combined. Set to one side.

Put the minced chicken in a pan with a little boiling salted water, then reduce the heat and simmer for 3 minutes or until cooked. Take off the heat and cool to room temperature.

Just before serving, add the roasted chilli powder and the rest of the chicken and crab combo ingredients and mix well. Check that the flavour is hot, salty and sour and add a few extra drops of lime juice, if necessary.

In a serving bowl, combine all the herbs, the cucumber, the cooked chicken and crab mix, the noodles and dressing, tossing together to mix. Sprinkle with the ground roast rice to serve.

Tip
To make your own roasted chilli powder, roast 2–3 whole dried red chillies in a 200°C/180°C fan/gas 6 oven for 5–10 minutes until dark brown. Pound them in a mortar and pestle until ground to a powder. Warning – this is seriously hot!

# PAJEON (KOREAN SEAFOOD AND SPRING ONION PANCAKES)

**SERVES 4**

1 teaspoon baking powder

150g self-raising flour

100g mixed fresh prawns and squid, finely chopped

3 tablespoons vegetable oil, plus extra for dribbling

5 spring onions, trimmed and quartered lengthways

*For the dipping sauce*

3 tablespoons rice vinegar

3 tablespoons soy sauce

½ teaspoon good-quality sesame oil

1 teaspoon sesame seeds

*There are classics and then there are classics, and this is a Korean classic.*

*This was taught to me at the Dongnae Halmae Pajeon restaurant on the outskirts of Seoul by a lady whose mother opened a restaurant in the 1960s where the only thing they made were these wonderful seafood pancakes ('halmae' means 'granny'!).*

In a large bowl, place 200ml cold water and the baking powder. Add the flour and mix to a batter – it should create a slightly thick pancake batter, similar to a drop scones batter. Add the seafood and stir.

Heat the vegetable oil in a frying pan over a high heat. Once the oil is hot, lay the spring onions in the pan, making an even rectangular layer like a net.

Pour the batter over the spring onions and fry for 2–3 minutes until the edges of the pancake are crispy and tiny air pockets have formed. Dribble a little oil on top of the pancake and flip. Flatten the pancake using a spatula and continue to cook for a further 3 minutes.

Meanwhile, mix together all the dipping sauce ingredients.

Once the pancake is crispy and golden on both sides, transfer to a plate and serve with the dipping sauce.

# POT STICKERS WITH VINEGAR DIPPING SAUCE

**MAKES ABOUT 18 POT STICKERS**

*For the pot stickers*

2 tablespoons vegetable oil, plus extra for greasing

1 garlic clove, grated

1 thumb-sized piece of fresh root ginger, peeled and grated

1 fresh red chilli, finely diced

6 small Thai shallots, finely chopped

50g carrots, peeled and very finely chopped

50g daikon radish, cut into julienne

50g Chinese cabbage leaves, finely chopped

50g firm tofu, crumbled

50g beansprouts, chopped

50g Chinese mushrooms, sliced

soy sauce and oyster sauce, to taste

a handful of chopped fresh coriander

18 gyoza wrappers

*For the vinegar dipping sauce*

2 tablespoons apple cider vinegar

2 tablespoons light soy sauce

1 tablespoon caster sugar

5 slices of white onion

*Now, what is the difference between a dumpling and a pot sticker? Well, a dumpling is soft all over and a pot sticker has a crunchy bottom and a steamed soft top. The way to cook pot stickers is a little tricky the first time, but after that your home will be pot sticker à go-go! These are vegetable ones, but many other varieties exist.*

Heat the vegetable oil in a wok, then fry the garlic, ginger, chilli and shallots slowly over a low heat until soft. Add the carrots, radish and cabbage, then add the tofu, beansprouts and mushrooms. Turn up the heat and stir-fry quickly to get a bit of crispy texture. Remove from the heat, transfer to a plate and leave to cool.

Once cool, season with the soy sauce and oyster sauce, then stir in the coriander.

To make the dipping sauce, put the vinegar, soy sauce, sugar and 1 tablespoon of water in a small pan and warm through over a low heat until the sugar has dissolved.

Pop the onion slices in a small heatproof bowl, pour over the warm liquid and leave to cool while you're making the dumplings.

For each pot sticker, put a teaspoon of the filling onto one half of a gyoza wrapper, wet the edges with water and fold it in half to make a half-moon shape, then seal and crimp the edges. Set to one side and repeat with the remaining filling and wrappers.

Brush a cold frying pan (with a lid) with vegetable oil, then place the dumplings in the cold pan in a Catherine wheel formation. Place the pan over a medium heat (this is the frying bit), then leave to colour for 2 minutes or until the bottoms of the dumplings are light brown.

Pour in 100ml water, then cover the pan and leave to steam for 2 minutes. Remove the lid and cook until all the water has evaporated and they start to fry and sizzle again. Serve immediately with the dipping sauce.

# SALADS

Hot, cold, sweet and spicy salads are lovely things full of texture and flavour. Not the first things you think of when it comes to Aussie or Asian food, but they are at the heart of both. In the West, a salad is more often a side, but in Asia it is usually a main or an equal partner in a spread of dishes. An Asian salad is a complex thing, with fine ingredients and sophisticated flavours. It's your lunch, dinner, even your breakfast.

# CRISP FRIED TOFU WITH SESAME AND PUMPKIN SEEDS AND PEA SHOOTS

## A GOOD SIDE SALAD FOR 6

300g firm tofu

50g cornflour

100ml vegetable oil, for frying

50g fresh pea shoots

20g pumpkin seeds, toasted

salt and freshly ground
white pepper

*For the dressing*

4 teaspoons vegetable oil

1 teaspoon good-quality
sesame oil

1 teaspoon sesame seeds

4 teaspoons light soy sauce

2 teaspoons apple
cider vinegar

salt and ground white pepper

*Tofu is so versatile and I wonder why it is not used more! Many people are a little scared I think, and don't know how to treat it. Cooking tofu is like cooking a piece of chicken – you can cook it any way you like, you can serve it with any sauce you want, it can be eaten hot or cold, and it's simple and delicious. This little salad is based on the crisp fried tofu you buy ready-done all over Asia.*

To make the dressing, put all the ingredients into a jam jar or similar, screw the lid on and shake until it's all mixed, then set to one side. It will keep in the fridge for a few days, so don't worry if you don't use it all.

Cut the tofu into strips about the size of your middle finger. Mix some salt and pepper into the cornflour in a dish, then roll the tofu pieces in it to coat all over.

Heat the vegetable oil in a heavy-based saucepan over a high heat and when shimmering, drop in a few pieces of tofu at a time and cook until the edges start to colour brown. Turn and cook the other side for a good 5 minutes or so until crisp and brown.

Remove and drain on kitchen paper, then repeat with the rest of the tofu until it's all crisp and brown, bringing the oil back up to temperature before frying the next batch.

Mix the tofu with the pea shoots and pumpkin seeds, then drizzle over some dressing, toss to mix well and serve.

# MALAY MIXED SALAD

. . . . . . . . . . . . . . . . . . . . . . . . . . . . . . . . . . . . . . . . . .

**SERVES 4**

*There are plenty of salads eaten all through Malaysia and this one includes a very different sambal recipe (or you can use a bought one). There will be plenty left over, but you can serve it alongside anything.*

. . . . . . . . . . . . . . . . . . . . . . . . . . . . . . . . . . . . . . . . . . . .

*For the dressing*

1 teaspoon belachan (shrimp paste), toasted (see Tip on page 138)

2 tablespoons sugar

2 tablespoons white vinegar

2 tablespoons fresh lemon juice

*For the salad*

1 cucumber, peeled and diced

1 fresh pineapple, peeled, cored and diced

1 green mango, peeled, seed removed and cut into strips

2 fresh red chillies, de-seeded and finely chopped

*For the hot shallot and lemongrass sambal*

10 small Thai shallots, diced

4 garlic cloves, finely diced

10 small fresh green chillies, minced

4 lime leaves, finely sliced

1 teaspoon belachan (shrimp paste), toasted

6 x 5cm lemongrass stalk lengths, outer leaves removed, minced

½ teaspoon salt

¼ teaspoon crushed black peppercorns

2 tablespoons fresh lime juice

80ml peanut oil

First make the sambal (see below).

Combine all the ingredients for the dressing in a food processor with 1 teaspoon of the sambal and blend together until smooth. Set the dressing to one side.

Put all the salad ingredients into a bowl and mix them together well. Now add a good 50ml of the dressing and toss together, then serve with extra dressing.

**Hot shallot and lemongrass sambal**

To make the sambal, combine all the ingredients together in a bowl, then transfer to a food processor and blend very quickly. Pour into a bowl and leave to sit for at least 1 hour to allow the flavours to blend.

Pour the sambal mix into a heavy-based saucepan and cook over a low heat for about 15 minutes, stirring occasionally, until fragrant and darker in colour.

Remove from the heat and set to one side until cool. Once cool, store in a jar in the fridge. It will keep for a couple of months.

# SPICED CRAB WITH GLASS NOODLES

**SERVES 4–6 AS A STARTER (OR UP TO 10 AS PART OF A BIGGER MEAL)**

*For the noodles*
a bunch of fresh coriander root, soaked and washed
200g minced chicken
1 teaspoon roasted chilli powder
2 small Thai shallots, finely sliced
juice of ½ lime
2 teaspoons fish sauce
250g glass noodles (mung bean thread or cellophane noodles)

*For the nam prik dressing*
2 dried red chillies, roasted (see Tip on page 184)
1 long fresh red and 1 long fresh green chilli, chopped
50g palm sugar
juice of ½ lime
2 tablespoons fish sauce

*For the salad*
1 cucumber, peeled
4 small Thai shallots, finely sliced
2 long fresh red chillies, finely sliced
a bunch of fresh Vietnamese mint, leaves picked
a bunch of fresh coriander leaves, leaves picked
a bunch of fresh round mint, leaves picked
a bunch of fresh Thai basil, leaves picked
200g crabmeat

*To serve*
a handful of roast rice (see Tip)

*Being a noodle dish doesn't mean it must be hot. In fact, many an Asian noodle dish is served cold, which Westerners usually classify as a salad (somehow we love to classify all sorts of things). Regardless, this is a showstopper, and although it takes a little time to make once you get all the shopping done, it's well worth the effort. Use any type of crab you like, but each variety will make the dish very different in flavour. Large crabs will be more sweet, small blue crabs more subtle and king crabs more salty.*

Pour 250ml water into a small pan. Add the coriander root and bring to a simmer. Add the minced chicken, chilli powder, shallots, lime juice and fish sauce and simmer gently for 5–10 minutes or until the chicken is cooked through. Put the glass noodles into a heatproof bowl and pour the chicken mixture over the top, then cover and set aside. Leave to soften for about 20 minutes, then use a pair of scissors to cut the noodles to desired lengths. Drain well, then set to one side to cool (discard the coriander root).

Using a mortar and pestle, pound the roasted chillies, fresh chillies and palm sugar together to a paste. Add the lime juice and fish sauce to taste and mix through. Add half the dressing to the noodle mix and toss to mix.

Cut the cucumber in half, remove the seeds and finely shred. In a large serving bowl, combine the cucumber, shallots and red chillies. Squeeze together the Vietnamese mint, coriander, round mint and Thai basil leaves, then tear the herbs and add to the bowl. Add the crabmeat, the noodle mixture and the remaining dressing to taste and toss through to combine.

Serve the salad with roast rice sprinkled over the top.

Tip
To make the roast rice, put some long grain rice into a heatproof bowl, cover with warm water and leave to soak for 20 minutes. Drain well, then transfer to a baking sheet and spread out evenly. Bake in a preheated oven at 200°C/180°C fan/gas 6 for 20 minutes until dry and crispy. Remove from the oven and pound it to break it up using a mortar and pestle. Leave to cool. Store in an airtight container (it will keep for several weeks).

# GRILLED COCONUT CHICKEN AND PEANUT SALAD

## FOR 6 TASTERS

### For the chicken

400ml tin coconut milk

2 tablespoons palm sugar

4 teaspoons fish sauce

6 skinless, boneless
   chicken thighs

### For the salad

2 small Thai shallots, sliced

2 long fresh red chillies, de-
   seeded and cut into julienne

2 teaspoons roasted peanuts,
   roughly chopped

½ cucumber, de-seeded and
   cut into julienne

a good handful of fresh
   coriander leaves

4 lime leaves, cut into very
   fine julienne

### To serve

6 banana leaves, each cut into
   a square shape

100g roasted peanuts, crushed
   into pieces

*Now this is a salad full of memories. The original version I ate in Sydney at David Thompson's Darley Street Thai, and then when I opened Mezzo, it was on as a starter served on shiny banana leaves. It's rich and sweet and fabulous. It is one of the few Thai dishes I know that is not at all spicy (well, it can be if you want to add more chilli!).*

Put the coconut milk, palm sugar and fish sauce into a saucepan and bring to the boil, then add the chicken, reduce to a simmer and poach it for 5 minutes. Remove from the heat and leave the chicken to cool in the liquid for at least 30 minutes.

Meanwhile, prepare the salad items and mix them all together in a bowl.

When the chicken is cool, remove it from the cooking liquid, reserving the liquid. Heat a griddle pan until it's really hot, then lift the poached thighs onto the griddle and cook over a high heat for 3 minutes on each side, until they have stripes of char.

Take the grilled chicken from the griddle and slice into thin strips, then drop it back into the coconut poaching liquid.

Remove the soaked chicken with a slotted spoon and drop it into the salad, then mix it all together.

Put a banana leaf (shiny green side up) onto the centre of each serving plate, then spoon the chicken mixture onto the banana leaves and dribble over some of the poaching liquid. Scatter the peanuts over the salad. Eat and enjoy!

# PEAR AND OKRA WITH COCONUT DRESSING

**SERVES 2**

1 lemon, halved

1 large nashi (Asian) pear
(or 2 crisp pears)

3 small fresh okra

1 fresh red chilli, de-seeded
and very finely diced

1 teaspoon good-quality
toasted sesame oil

400ml tin coconut milk

salt

*The raw okra and pear react here with the coconut milk, the milk thickens and the whole thing becomes an amazing salad of thick pear and coconut chilli deliciousness.*

*When I travel I am very fortunate to meet many talented people. This recipe comes from my trip to Korea and working with one of the country's up-and-coming young chefs. He had taken the principles of Buddhist temple food and made a modern and very beautiful dish where the pear takes the place of noodles. There is no garlic or onion in this dish, as they are never used in temple food because they stir emotion…*

Fill a bowl with cold water and squeeze the lemon juice into it. Quarter the pear and remove the core with a sharp knife, then, using a mandolin, slice it very thinly, dropping the slices into the lemon water as you go.

Trim the okra and slice very thinly.

Drain the pear slices, then mix with the okra and chilli in a bowl. Sprinkle over the sesame oil. Pour over the coconut milk, sprinkle a little salt on top, then leave for 5 minutes.

Eat and enjoy.

# PORK LAAP

. . . . . . . . . . . . . . . . . . . . . . . . . . . . . . . . .

**ENOUGH FOR 2**

300g finely minced pork

2 tablespoons fish sauce

90ml fresh lime juice

8 small Thai shallots, sliced

a handful of fresh mint

a handful of fresh coriander

3 teaspoons roasted
chilli powder

2 small fresh red chillies, sliced

a few large sprigs of fresh
Thai basil

fried sticky rice (see Tip)

⅛ round Asian cabbage (or
iceberg lettuce), separated
into leaves

*Laap, Laab or Larp, or whichever way you would like to spell it, is addictive in the most wonderful of ways. I have eaten this in many a place on many a street corner and in many a restaurant all across the world. I still love the ones that are made on the streets late at night in humid Bangkok, and it must be 'pet pet', hot and spicy, or 'pet ma', meaning very spicy. Hot and salty, it is served with lots of herbs on their stems and some Asian cabbage on the side, so you can just indulge.*

. . . . . . . . . . . . . . . . . . . . . . . . . . . . . . . . . . . . . . . . . . .

Heat a wok over a medium heat, then add the pork with 4 teaspoons of salted water and simmer for 3 minutes or until cooked, stirring occasionally to break it up. Remove from the heat and cool to room temperature.

Just before serving, add the fish sauce, lime juice, shallots, mint, coriander, chilli powder and chillies to the cooked pork and mix well. Taste and check that the flavour is hot, salty and sour. Add a few extra drops of lime juice to sharpen and define the flavour if you want to.

Serve the pork with the Thai basil and sticky rice on the side and the cabbage to scoop it all up with.

Tip
To make fried sticky rice, take 50g cooked rice of any type. Spread out on a baking sheet, keeping the rice in clumps, and cook in a preheated 150°C/130°C fan/gas 2 oven for 20 minutes to dry out. Heat 100ml vegetable oil in a wok or heavy-based saucepan until it reaches 180°C. The oil will start to shimmer when ready. Scatter the rice into the hot oil – it will puff up as it fries and start to go light brown. Turn and cook so it is the same colour all over, about 5 minutes, then remove with a spider (skimmer) and drain on kitchen paper.

Back shopping in the market with Khun Pip (see my diary, page 8) almost twenty-five years after first meeting her! She still runs the Thai House, a fabulous cookery school and guest house in a village just outside Bangkok.

# MISO BAKED AUBERGINE WITH BROWN RICE SALAD

**FOR 4 AS A STARTER**

*For the rice*

100g brown rice

2 x 20g packets of miso
   soup mix

2 spring onions, chopped

20g alfalfa sprouts

*For the aubergines*

2 large aubergines

100g white miso paste

4 teaspoons mirin

4 teaspoons vegetable oil

*For the dressing*

50ml light soy sauce

1 teaspoon caster sugar

4 tablespoons rice vinegar

2 tablespoons sake

1 long fresh red chilli,
   finely diced

2 teaspoons peanut oil

*Aubergine has become a trendy vegetable, but I have always been a fan. One of the easiest ways to cook it is to bake it. This method is failsafe, and should you simply want to do baked aubergines and pesto, use pesto instead of miso. The brown rice is easy enough, but soak it in cold water for 30 minutes before cooking and you will get a better result. Well, I do anyway.*

Soak the rice in cold water for 30 minutes, then drain.

Preheat the oven to 200°C/180°C fan/gas 6.

Take a baking sheet, cut the aubergines in half lengthways and place on the sheet. Score the flesh in a criss-cross pattern, making cuts about 3cm apart. Mix the white miso with the mirin and oil and then spread this over the cut sides of the aubergines, using a quarter of the mix on each half. Pop into the oven and bake for 25 minutes or until soft all the way through (the sides will start to collapse).

Put the drained rice into a pot with the miso soup mixes and 200ml water. Bring to the boil and place a lid on the pot, then reduce the heat and leave to simmer for 6 minutes. Don't lift the lid, but turn the heat off and leave the rice to sit, undisturbed, for at least 25 minutes.

Lift the lid and add the spring onions, forking them through – there should not be any liquid left, as it should all have been absorbed, and the rice should now be cooked all the way through. Pour onto a flat tray and leave to cool, then mix in the alfalfa sprouts.

Mix all the dressing ingredients together in a small bowl.

Serve the cooked rice salad and baked aubergine halves, hot or cold, with the dressing drizzled over.

# SWEET BASIL SALAD
# WITH FENNEL, CORIANDER AND CHILLI

**SERVES 4**

1 fennel bulb, finely shaved, ideally on a mandolin

2 tablespoons fresh lime juice, plus extra to taste

½ teaspoon salt

4 tablespoons olive oil

2 fresh red chillies, de-seeded and cut into julienne

4 spring onions, finely sliced diagonally

a small handful of fresh coriander leaves

a small handful of fresh Thai or regular basil leaves

a small handful of fresh mint leaves

a handful of crispy fried onions

salt and freshly ground black pepper

*This is a salad that combines the tastes of Asia and Sydney. As a young man, I cooked this as a stand-alone salad and also often mixed it with finely shaved squid, a piece of grilled fish or some seared scallops. It's a real old-style fusion salad and takes me back many years.*

Mix the fennel with 1 tablespoon of the lime juice and the salt and set aside for 30 minutes.

Warm the olive oil in a small frying pan, then add the chillies and spring onions. Toss for 30 seconds, then remove from the heat and add the remaining lime juice. Set aside for 30 minutes.

Combine the marinated fennel with the chillies and spring onions, and stir well.

Combine the coriander, basil and mint leaves and toss together, then fold them into the fennel mixture. Transfer to a large serving dish and sprinkle with the crispy fried onions. Season with salt and black pepper and extra lime juice to taste, if needed.

# LAMB SALAD WITH BEANSPROUTS AND CHILLI

........................................................................

**ENOUGH FOR 6**

200g trimmed lamb fillets or a 200g loin of lamb

50ml vegetable oil

10 lime leaves, cut into julienne

3 long fresh red chillies, cut into julienne

a good handful of fresh coriander leaves

a good handful of fresh Thai basil leaves

100g beansprouts

*For the dressing*

50ml fresh lime juice

50ml vegetable oil

2 tablespoons fish sauce

1 small fresh red chilli, finely diced

2 garlic cloves, sliced

*This is a quick and delicious salad. I used to call it my Thai lamb salad until I understood that the Thais don't eat lamb because they believe it smells; their loss, I say. I used to use little lamb fillets as they would be left over from other dishes in the restaurant, and if you can find them, do use them as they are lean and cook very quickly. The secret is to toss the salad whilst the lamb is warm so everything wilts and blends and becomes one.*

........................................................................

Heat a heavy-based pan over a high heat. Rub the lamb all over with the vegetable oil and then sear it quickly on both sides – the fillets take just a few minutes; the loin will take a good 8–10 minutes. Remove the lamb to a plate and leave to rest for 5 minutes.

Meanwhile, combine all the dressing ingredients in a small bowl, mixing together well.

Slice the lamb thinly, then put into a bowl with the cooking juices, the lime leaves, chillies and herbs and toss through. Add the beansprouts and a tablespoon of the dressing and toss to mix.

Serve on individual plates or in a big bowl and dribble the remaining dressing over.

# CRISPY CANDIED NOODLES

. . . . . . . . . . . . . . . . . . . . . . . . . . . . . . . . . . .

**MAKES 4 LITTLE BOWLFULS**

150g dried thin or thick
rice noodles

300ml vegetable oil, plus extra
for the noodles

1 garlic clove, sliced

1 small Thai shallot, sliced

50g minced pork

100g peeled fresh raw prawns,
finely chopped

1 tablespoon fermented soya
beans (optional)

1 tablespoon rice vinegar

1 tablespoon fish sauce

30g palm sugar

1 teaspoon roasted
chilli powder

1 tablespoon fresh lime juice
and 1 tablespoon lime zest

2 pickled garlic cloves,
finely sliced

a small bunch of fresh
coriander, chopped

1 long fresh red chilli,
thinly sliced

60g beansprouts

3 Chinese chives, chopped

*This might sound a bit out there, because it is. Noodles that are crisp,
with a sticky sweet-and-salty sauce across the top. Well, we have prawn
cocktail and cheese and onion crisps, so why not?!*

. . . . . . . . . . . . . . . . . . . . . . . . . . . . . . . . . . . . . . . . . . . . . . . . . . .

If the noodles are very fine, fry them in a little vegetable oil in a frying
pan until crisp and golden brown, then drain on kitchen paper. If the
noodles are thick, soak them in water for 15 minutes, then drain well and
fry a few at a time as above until they are all cooked and crisp. Set them
to one side.

Heat 50ml of the vegetable oil in a frying pan until hot. Fry the garlic
and shallot for a few minutes until fragrant, then add the pork and
prawns, seasoning the mix with the fermented soya beans, vinegar, fish
sauce, palm sugar and chilli powder. Bring to the boil and cook for a few
minutes until thick, then add the lime juice. Mix and adjust the seasoning
so it's sweet, sour and salty.

Reduce the heat, add the fried noodles and continue stirring them in the
sauce until they stick together.

Spoon the sticky noodles onto serving plates. Sprinkle with the pickled
garlic, lime zest, coriander and fresh chilli. Place the beansprouts and
chopped Chinese chives along the sides of the plates to eat with the
crisp noodle salad.

# DUCK AND WATERMELON SALAD

**ENOUGH FOR 4 PEOPLE**

*Due to the sorts of ingredients that are in this Asian salad, I have given you rough amounts by handfuls and tablespoons rather than by weight.*

2 duck breasts

salt, to taste

½ daikon radish

1 carrot

1 pomelo

3 spring onions, sliced into long strips

a handful of water chestnuts, sliced

3 handfuls of watermelon, cut into thumb-sized chunks

a good handful of fresh coriander leaves

a good handful of fresh Thai basil leaves

4 cos lettuces

Fried Garnish (see page 204)

*For the dressing*

1 fresh red and 1 fresh green Thai chilli

2 tablespoons palm sugar

1 tablespoon concentrated cooking tamarind

2 tablespoons fish sauce

2 tablespoons lime juice

First cook the duck. Score the skin of the duck very well, all the way through to the flesh, then trim any sinew from the duck flesh.

Put the breast into a cold frying pan skin-side down and season with a little salt. Cook slowly for 5 minutes so that the fat melts and the skin is crisp. Turn over and spoon with the fat as the duck cooks. Leave to rest, then slice as thinly as possible.

Make the dressing by crushing the chillies, sugar and tamarind in a mortar and pestle and pounding to a paste, then add the fish sauce and lime juice and continue to pound until the dressing is well mixed.

Shred the daikon and carrot, preferably on a mandolin, into thin strips about 6cm long and 2.5mm wide. Prepare the pomelo by peeling it and then segmenting. Discard the peel and the bits that are not just fruit. Mix the daikon, carrot and pomelo together with the spring onions, water chestnuts and watermelon, then add the herbs.

Take the cos lettuces and run cold water over them to make crisp. Remove the two outer leaves and discard, then peel the leaves away one at a time until you get to the smaller ones, which you can keep for another salad.

Mix the dressing with the duck and all the vegetables and serve topped with the crispy fried garnish. Serve the lettuce leaves on the side to use as wraps.

# WON-DROUS WOK

And what a wondrous thing it is. It can steam, it can fry, it can bake, it can poach and stir-fry and it can even be used as a hat when the tropical rains come and you are caught out in a downpour. The most inexpensive cooking pot you'll ever buy, invest in a good-sized one, look after it and it'll last you a lifetime.

# PEPPERED TOFU WITH AUBERGINE

**FOR 4–6 PEOPLE**

300g Japanese or Thai
fragrant rice

*For the topping*

2 aubergines, each cut into
12 chunks

20g black peppercorns

200g firm tofu

2 tablespoons peanut or
corn oil

4 spring onions, green part
only, chopped

2 garlic cloves, grated

1 thumb-sized piece of
fresh root ginger, peeled
and grated

2 tablespoons mirin

2 tablespoons dark soy sauce

250ml hot water

salt

*Quick and easy and a proper stir-fry. Cook the rice while preparing the
ingredients for the tofu and aubergine topping.*

Boil, steam or cook the rice in an electric rice cooker or see page 182 for
Perfect Rice.

Heat the wok with 250ml of water and drop in the aubergine. Bring to
the boil and cook, stirring occasionally, for 5 minutes until soft.

In the meantime, pound the peppercorns in a mortar and pestle until
fine, then sieve through a fine sieve. The larger black bits will be left in
the sieve and these are used to coat the tofu, while the other sieved part
is the white and very hot pepper used to season later.

Cut the tofu into matchbox-sized chunks and roll in the black pepper.

Drain the aubergines, put to one side and dry the wok.

Heat the oil in the wok, add the peppered tofu and cook for 3 minutes.
Add the spring onions, garlic and ginger. Keep the heat high and stir for
a minute or two until fragrant. Add the aubergine and mix in well, then
add the mirin and soy sauce along with 250ml hot water.

Increase the heat and let the mixture boil vigorously for 1 minute. Taste
and add salt if necessary, then season with the sieved pepper mix to
make it hotter if you like it spicy. Serve with rice.

# WOK-FRIED MONKFISH

**ENOUGH FOR 4 WITH SOME RICE OR NOODLES**

500g monk cheeks or chunks of monkfish, cleaned

20g cornflour

100ml vegetable oil, for frying

1 large thumb-sized piece of fresh root ginger, peeled and grated

5 garlic cloves, grated

100g beansprouts

100g mangetout or sugar snap peas

200g baby corn

100g carrots, peeled and cut diagonally

200g Chinese cabbage leaves

6 spring onions, chopped

50ml dark soy sauce

50ml oyster sauce

salt

noodles or rice, to serve

2 handfuls of fresh coriander leaves, to garnish

*The secret to any stir-fry is the speed at which it is cooked. This means that the heat must be high and the wok not lifted away from the flame, but shuffled over the heat. Preparation is essential for a good crispy stir-fry. Get everything ready, including your serving plate, because once the cooking is underway, it's non-stop until it hits the plate.*

Dust the fish with the cornflour and season with a little salt.

Heat the wok over a high heat. When it is hot, pour in half the oil and heat until it shimmers. Add half the monkfish and cook until light brown. Take from the wok and repeat the process, keeping the cooked fish to one side.

After cooking the monkfish, discard the oil that is in the wok and wipe it clean with a cloth. Put it back on the heat and get it really hot, then add the remaining oil, the ginger and the garlic. Give it a stir and then add all the vegetables – the wok MUST be hot. Stir and move the vegetables a little so they start to soften and the colours brighten. Put the monkfish back in and then add soy and oyster sauce to taste. The stir-fry is ready when the vegetables are crisp but not raw and the fish not overcooked but firm.

Serve with rice or noodles, either on the side or pour the mix over the top. Garnish with coriander leaves.

# GREEN BEANS, CHILLI AND SESAME SEEDS

**A SIDE FOR 2**

200g green beans

2 teaspoons vegetable oil

1 banana shallot, finely diced

2 long fresh red chillies,
  finely chopped

2 tablespoons sesame seeds

4 teaspoons dark soy sauce

*Green beans in Thailand are long and a little more chewy than the ones we use. If you can find these snake (yard long) beans, boil them for a minute or two longer than these ones before adding them to the wok.*

Blanch the beans in boiling water for literally 30 seconds, then drain. Whilst the beans cook, heat your wok.

Add the oil and when it's hot, add the shallot and then the hot wet beans – they will sizzle, be careful.

Add the chilli and the sesame seeds and stir. Keep the heat up and cook until the shallot starts to colour and the seeds start to pop. Take from the heat and add the dark soy, give it all a stir and serve.

Back in Thailand buying basil at Nonthaburi market, wandering through the temple in Bangkok that is the burial site of the real king from *The King and I* and a view of the Chao Phraya River from my hotel room.

# PAD PRIK KING WITH SQUID

. . . . . . . . . . . . . . . . . . . . . . . . . . . . . . . . . . .

**SERVES 4 (WITH
OTHER DISHES)**

100g pork fat (or about 120ml
    vegetable oil)

vegetable oil, for frying

100g palm sugar

5 teaspoons fish sauce

300g medium-sized squid,
    cleaned

10–15 lime leaves

a good handful of fresh
    Thai basil

*For the paste*

6 large dried red chillies

9 large fresh red
    (serrano) chillies

30g dried shrimps, soaked
    (see Tip on page 154)

pared rind of ¼ lime

1 teaspoon salt

6 fresh coriander roots, soaked
    and washed, then chopped

6 small Thai shallots, chopped

10 garlic cloves, peeled

a big fat thumb-sized piece of
    fresh galangal, chopped

3 lemongrass stalks, outer
    leaves removed and inner
    leaves shredded

*This is one of my all-time favourites, and the starting point for what became 'lucky squid', which sat proudly on my menus for over 15 years; how time flies.*

*Some things translate and some do not. In Thai, the translation of 'king' is ginger. Ironically there is no ginger in this recipe, and on a recent trip to Thailand when I asked my cooking teacher why was it called king, but contained no king, they looked at me and said they had no idea and had never even thought about it. I guess there are no cottages in a cottage pie, either.*

. . . . . . . . . . . . . . . . . . . . . . . . . . . . . . . . . . . . . . . . . . . . . . . .

First make the paste. Snap the stalk end from the dried red chillies and shake out the seeds. Put the dried chillies into a bowl and cover with hot water. Leave for about 20 minutes until they have plumped up.

Slit the fresh chillies down the centre with a sharp knife and use the handle of a small spoon like a shovel to push out all the seeds, then chop the chillies.

Drain the hydrated chillies and shrimps, then put them into a food processor with all the other paste ingredients and process (or pound them in a mortar with a pestle) until you have a rough paste. You may need to add a little water to bring the paste together, but try to add as little as possible as the ingredients, particularly the soaked chillies and shrimps, will contain their own moisture.

Heat the pork fat (or vegetable oil) in a heavy-based saucepan and add the paste. Cook it very slowly, taking care that it doesn't catch on the bottom of the pan, for about 40 minutes until all the moisture disappears.

Halfway through cooking, add the palm sugar and 3 teaspoons of the fish sauce. When the paste is ready, it will be very aromatic and the colour will have deepened to a rich red-brown. Take it off the heat and keep it on one side until you are ready to cook your squid.

To prepare the squid, slit the bodies lengthways and open out into sheets. Place, insides upwards, on a chopping board. Using a very sharp knife or a cleaver at a 45-degree angle, score the squid almost through diagonally one way in a series of cuts about 5mm apart, then turn the squid round and repeat at right angles to the first cuts, so you finish up with a diamond pattern. Cut each squid body into decent-sized pieces (about 6 x 4cm).

Continues on the next page…

. . . . . . . . . . . . . . . . . . . . . . . . . . . . . . .

# PAD PRIK KING WITH SQUID
(continued)

Now get a wok really hot and add a film of vegetable oil. When the oil is really hot, put in the squid pieces, scored side downwards, with the tentacles if you are using them. The secret is to leave the squid pieces for a moment to seal before attempting to move them. They will colour slightly and curl up completely to resemble small fir cones. If the oil isn't hot enough, the squid won't cook quickly enough and liquid may leach out. If this happens, drain off the liquid and put the wok straight back on the heat.

Add about 2 tablespoons of your paste to the wok, together with the remaining fish sauce, and stir everything around well to coat the squid.

Fold the lime leaves in half and pull out the stalks, which are too stringy to eat raw, then chop the leaves quite finely. Chop the basil. Sprinkle both on top of the squid and serve immediately with more of the paste on the side.

Tip
To store the leftover paste, cool it, then pop it into a jar and keep in the fridge for up to a month. It's very nice on toast!

# KOREAN FRIED CHICKEN

1kg chicken pieces (preferably
a whole chicken, cut into
16 pieces)
500ml vegetable oil, for
deep-frying
sesame seeds, to garnish

*For the chicken seasoning*
2 tablespoons potato starch
(cornflour)
2 tablespoons gochugaru
(Korean ground chilli)
1 tablespoon minced garlic
1 tablespoon salt
1 teaspoon ground white
pepper

*For the batter*
6 tablespoons potato starch
3 tablespoons sweet rice flour
3 tablespoons plain flour
1 teaspoon baking powder
½ teaspoon salt
½ teaspoon ground white
pepper
200ml soju

*For the sticky chilli sauce*
8 tablespoons rice syrup (or
agave syrup)
5 tablespoons gochujang
(Korean chilli paste)
1 teaspoon minced garlic
5 tablespoons apple or
rice vinegar
1 tablespoon gochugaru
(Korean ground chilli)

*For the pickled moo*
2 tablespoons rice vinegar
1 tablespoon caster sugar
300g Korean radish (moo) or
daikon radish, scrubbed and
cut into 1cm cubes

*Thinking I had perfected my Korean Fried Chicken recipe some years ago
and even published it, I then went to Korea. There I ate many versions,
some without sauce (not right!) and even a version that was just bones.
So, having been inspired and reeducated, here it is, JT's Korean Fried
Chicken. MKII. The sauce is called yangnyeom (or, as I call it, 'yum yum').
I am confident I have now created a proper Korean Fried Chicken recipe.*

*The first word I learnt to read in Korean was dak, which means 'chicken',
and the symbols that translate it are Ct27 (well that's how I remember it).
So if you're in Korea and you see Ct27, chicken is not far away, and beer,
as beer and chicken are called Chimaek, chi for 'chicken' and maekju for
'beer', and are always together like love and marriage... MKII.*

Take the chicken pieces and slash the skin in places – this will help the
batter to stick and the chicken to be crisp.

Heat the vegetable oil in a wok to 170°C (if you drop in a little batter, it
should sizzle and float).

Mix together the chicken seasoning ingredients in a large bowl, drop in
the pieces and lightly coat them all over.

Mix all the dry batter ingredients in a separate large bowl, then add
200ml of soju and 200ml of water until you have a smooth batter, about
the thickness of single cream.

Dip the chicken in the batter and coat it well, shaking off the excess.
Gently drop the pieces into the hot oil about six pieces at a time, so you
don't overcrowd the fryer. Deep-fry for 8–10 minutes until golden. Pick
the chicken out of the oil and put on a cake cooling rack, then leave to
rest for 10 minutes. Repeat the frying until all the chicken is cooked.

Mix all the chilli sauce ingredients together in a saucepan and simmer
over a medium heat for 5 minutes, then take from the stove and leave.

The pickle is easy – mix the rice vinegar, sugar and 2 tablespoons water in
a bowl. Add the cubed moo, stir and set to one side.

When all the chicken has been cooked the first time, reheat the oil to
170°C and re-fry a few pieces at a time for 5–6 minutes so they are really
crispy! When ready, drain on the rack again.

Now, it's up to you how you serve: pickle and sauce on the side, some
dipped in, some not, sprinkled with sesame seeds, whatever you like.

*Pictures also on pages 116–117*

# SALT AND PEPPER DUCK, PLUM SAUCE AND PANCAKES

**FEEDS 4**

**For the duck**

4 duck breasts, trimmed

2 teaspoons salt flakes

2 teaspoons black peppercorns

80g self-raising flour

150ml vegetable oil, for frying

**To serve**

Plum Sauce (see opposite)

shredded spring onions

shredded cucumber

beansprouts

pancakes

*I decided to create my own recipe for this iconic dish as I wanted to make something accessible using the spices and flavours of the classic duck and plum sauce. The recipe is quick and easy, but should you not have time to make the plum sauce, then simply buy a bottle or use hoisin instead. The process of cooking the duck is also delicious done with chicken, pork or beef fillet.*

Take the duck breasts, place them skin-side down on a chopping board and cut lengthways into thin strips, as thin as you possibly can.

Take the salt and the peppercorns and grind together in a mortar and pestle, then add the flour to the salt and pepper mix.

Put the duck into a large mixing bowl and throw over the spiced flour, giving it all a good tumble to coat it, then leave to sit. This helps to make a coating on the duck as the duck will soak up the flour.

Heat a wok with half the oil. When the oil is shimmering, add half the duck, carefully dropping each piece in separately. Leave to fry and sizzle for a minute, then turn and repeat twice, keeping the oil hot. The pieces will be crispy and will curl a little. Remove the duck and discard the oil, then repeat with the remaining duck and oil.

Serve with the Plum Sauce, shredded spring onion, cucumber, beansprouts and pancakes.

*Pictures also on pages 120–123*

# PLUM SAUCE

## MAKES A JAR

2 teaspoons vegetable oil

1 shallot, peeled
   and diced

1 garlic clove, crushed

1 thumb-sized piece of
   fresh root ginger, peeled
   and grated

60ml white vinegar

2 tins plums, drained and cut
   into wedges

*For the spices*

pinch each of black pepper,
   cinnamon and cloves

1 teaspoon Chinese
   five-spice powder

½ teaspoon sugar

*As plums are not always available, the sensible thing to do is to use tinned plums.*

Put the oil and the shallot into a heavy-based saucepan and cook for a couple of minutes over a high heat. Add the garlic and ginger, reduce the heat and cook a little until fragrant.

Add the spices and sugar and cook for 30 seconds. Next, add the vinegar and stand back as it will boil and is very strong. Finally, add the plums and give everything a good stir. Bring to the boil and cook for 5 minutes, then mash with a fork, bring to the boil again and cook for a good 5 minutes until it is a thick sauce consistency.

# WHOLE STEAMED SEA BASS, GINGER AND SPRING ONIONS

**FOR 2 OR 4 THOUGH I HAVE BEEN KNOWN TO EAT A WHOLE ONE MYSELF – GREEDY GUTS!**

800g whole sea bass or sea bream

75ml Chinese (Shaoxing) rice wine (or sherry)

150ml light soy sauce

30g caster sugar

100g fresh root ginger, peeled and cut into julienne

50g spring onions, white and green parts kept separate, cut into julienne

4 teaspoons good-quality sesame oil

4 teaspoons peanut oil

*Steamed fish in a wok? Really? Well, the reason is that it is the easiest way to make this classic Hong Kong dish. There are not many ingredients, but the fish is always soft and delicious and falls off the bone. In Hong Kong, this is the dish that everyone hankers for – it's the cottage pie of Kowloon!*

Pat the fish dry with a tea towel and place on a chopping board. Make three slits into the fish from head to tail at an angle, turn the fish 90 degrees and make three more cuts to create a diamond pattern. Repeat on the other side of the fish. This helps the fish to cook more evenly.

In a small saucepan, mix together the wine and the soy and add the sugar, stirring until it is dissolved.

Heat your wok with a good 2 cups of water and pop a little rack in the bottom. Take a large oval plate that will fit in the wok and sprinkle with half the ginger and half the white spring onions.

Pop the fish on top and finish with the remaining ginger and the whites of the spring onions (the greens are kept for later). Pour over the sauce.

Lift the plate carefully into the wok and put a lid on top. Steam until the flesh of the fish is firm, about 10–12 minutes, and remove from the steamer.

Sprinkle with the green parts of the spring onions. In a little pan, heat the two oils until smoking and pour over the steamed fish, setting the spring onion alive.

Serve with steamed rice.

# CRISPY PORK AND XO SAUCE

........................................................

**SERVES 4 WITH OTHER DISHES**

500g boned pork leg or neck (skin and fat attached)

100ml vegetable oil

200g gai lan or tenderstem broccoli

1 tablespoon palm sugar

1 tablespoon fish sauce

3 tablespoons XO Sauce (see the recipe below or open a jar)

a handful of fresh basil, chopped

*For the XO sauce*

6 large dried scallops

20g large dried shrimps

100g fresh long red chillies, de-seeded and chopped

1 thumb-sized piece of fresh root ginger, peeled and chopped

5 garlic cloves, chopped

100ml vegetable oil

3 teaspoons sea salt

3 teaspoons caster sugar

*You can buy XO sauce, so there is no need to make it, but it is very satisfying! Once you have made your own, play with the recipe and work out if you would like it to be stronger with chilli or sweeter or maybe with more flavour of the sea. I love XO with scallops or crisp chicken and even with dumplings, but this sticky pork I made recently in Hong Kong, the birthplace of XO, went down a storm with the crew and locals alike.*

........................................................

Cut the pork into two pieces, keeping the skin on (this is really important). Put the pieces into a steamer and cook for 25 minutes, then take from the steamer and leave to cool a little. Slice the pork into really thin strips, thinner than a slice of bread, still keeping the skin on.

Put half the vegetable oil in a wok and bring it up to a good heat. Fry half the pork until the skin is really golden and crispy and the pork properly heated through, about 10 minutes (it will pop a bit). Remove and drain. Repeat with the remaining oil and pork.

Drain off the excess oil from the wok, then add the gai lan with the palm sugar and fish sauce and cook for 5 minutes or until just tender.

Put all the pork back into the wok with the gai lan and bring the dish together with 3 tablespoons or so of the XO sauce. Stir it around until it is well heated through – it should be sticky and hot and sweet. Scatter with the chopped basil to serve.

## XO sauce

Soak the dried scallops and the dried shrimps in warm water for 2 hours.

Blend all the ingredients together, adding the seafood first and then the other bits.

Put into a heavy-based pan and cook slowly over a low heat for a good 45 minutes, stirring often.

Pour into a jar and store for up to a month.

# DAK GALBI (SPICY CHICKEN STEW)

**SERVES 2**

500g chicken thigh fillets

150g tteok (long Korean
rice cakes)

1 tablespoon vegetable oil

1 medium sweet potato, cut
into chunky chips

2 carrots, peeled and sliced

¼ cabbage, cut into
medium-sized chunks

2 spring onions, finely chopped

2 perilla leaves (or a mix of Thai
and regular basil)

*For the marinade*

3 tablespoons gochujang
(Korean chilli paste)

2 tablespoons gochugaru
(Korean ground chilli)

3 tablespoons mirin or Korean
rice wine

3 tablespoons sugar

1 teaspoon minced fresh
root ginger

½ teaspoon minced garlic

3 tablespoons soy sauce

pinch of finely ground
black pepper

1 tablespoon Korean curry
powder (or medium
curry powder)

*This is a very clever and very quick one-wok wonder. It really is simple, simple, simple.*

Mix the marinade ingredients together to make a thick paste. Cut the chicken thighs into bite-sized pieces and add, mixing well so they are all coated. Leave for 30 minutes.

If the rice cakes are fresh, then skip this step, otherwise if they are hard, soak them in enough warm water to cover for 30 minutes, then drain.

Heat the oil in a wok over a high heat. Add the chicken and the marinade and when it begins to boil, turn it down to medium and cook for 5–6 minutes.

Add the sweet potato, carrot, rice cakes and cabbage in layers on top of the chicken mixture and allow to steam a little. Stir them into the sauce and cook until the vegetables are soft and the rice cakes have plumped up.

Just before serving, turn the heat off, add the spring onions and finely chopped perilla leaves to the sauce and stir in.

Serve the stew with rice, kimchi, seaweed and danmuji (yellow pickled radish) or daikon radish on the side.

# QUICK LAKSA

......................................

**FEEDS 2 HUNGRY PEOPLE**

*For the laksa paste*
50g galangal, roughly chopped
50g fresh root ginger, peeled
   and roughly chopped
2 garlic cloves, peeled
50g belachan (shrimp paste),
   toasted (see Tip on
   page 138)
10 small Thai shallots,
   roughly chopped
3 lemongrass stalks, outer
   leaves removed and inner
   leaves roughly chopped
10 fresh coriander stalks
2 fresh long red chillies,
   de-seeded
2 tablespoons fish sauce
4 lime leaves, cut into julienne
2 tablespoons vegetable oil

*For the soup*
1–2 tablespoons vegetable oil
1 litre light vegetable stock
50ml coconut milk
1 tablespoon fish sauce
300g pre-cooked fresh
   white noodles
20g beansprouts

50g choy sum, sliced
50g Chinese cabbage, cut
   into julienne
50g tofu, cut and deep-fried
   (you can fry it yourself or buy
   already deep-fried)
½ cucumber, de-seeded and
   cut into julienne
a handful of fresh coriander
   leaves
sambal oelek, to serve

*Laksa is a bowl of spiced noodle soup. It does take time to make and there are many parts, but it is a wonderful dish. As the world changes, so does the laksa. It will be different in every region as you travel, so if this is not like the one you've had before, good, give it a try.*

......................................

Blend all the paste ingredients except the oil in a food processor, then fry the paste over a low heat in the vegetable oil for 10 minutes. This can be made in advance.

To make the soup, heat the oil in a wok and add 2 tablespoons of the paste. Cook for 3 minutes, then add the stock and coconut milk.

Bring the soup to the boil and season with fish sauce. Add the noodles to the soup, bring up to the boil and add the beansprouts.

Pour into a bowl and garnish with the choy sum, cabbage, tofu, cucumber and some coriander leaves. Serve the sambal oelek on the side.

# CRISP FRIED PIGEON, CELERIAC PURÉE AND SZECHUAN GUNPOWDER

....................................................

## FOR 4

4 pigeons, trimmed

1 lemon, cut into 4 wedges

vegetable oil, for deep-frying

*For the Szechuan gunpowder*

30g Szechuan peppercorns

90g table salt

*For the master stock*

200ml Chinese (Shaoxing)
    rice wine

100ml light soy sauce

50ml dark soy sauce

100g yellow rock sugar

50g cassia bark

100g piece of fresh root ginger

4 garlic cloves

2 spring onions

*For the celeriac purée*

½ celeriac, peeled and diced

1 large potato, peeled
    and diced

½ apple, peeled, cored
    and diced

100ml milk

50g butter

salt and freshly ground
    black pepper

*Sometimes you have to go a bit out of your way to cook something new and a little different. Throughout this book I have tried where possible to do what I call crowd pleasers or familiar dishes. This is not one of those BUT it is one of my prized recipes, developed over many, many years with a little help from my cheffy friends. A recipe inspired by Asia and cooked in a true Sydney style.*

....................................................

In a dry pan, roast the Szechuan pepper with the salt until smoky and dark in colour. Grind in a mortar and pestle or blitz in a food processor.

Bring all the master stock ingredients up to the boil with 2 litres of water. Push a lemon wedge into each pigeon and simmer for 10 minutes.

Remove the pigeons from the stock and let cool a little.

For the celeriac purée, combine all the ingredients in a saucepan, topping the milk up with water to just cover. Cook over a medium heat for about 15 minutes to reduce the liquid and until the celeriac is cooked. Strain the purée, reserving the liquid. Blitz in a food processor, adding the liquid slowly until the mixture is smooth and you have the consistency you want.

Heat the oil in a wok to 180°C. Deep-fry the pigeons two at a time until dark red. Take the legs and breasts off the carcasses.

Serve the pigeon pieces on the reheated celeriac purée, sprinkling the pigeon with Szechuan gunpowder.

Tip
You can reuse the master stock for poaching or braising chicken, duck or pork.

# SON-IN-LAW EGGS

SERVES 2

125g palm sugar

50ml fish sauce

20ml concentrated
cooking tamarind

100ml vegetable oil

4 eggs, hard boiled
and shelled

a handful of fresh
coriander leaves

Fried Garnish (see page 204)

*There are two stories for this – one that a mother-in-law loved her son-in-law so much that she cooked him this delight, and the other, less pleasant, that the son-in-law had been unfaithful and she cooked this dish to demonstrate how she would deal with him. He being the egg! First she would boil the egg/him, then remove the skin and plunge into boiling oil, frying until blistered and crispy. And lastly she would make a sauce of boiling palm sugar and pour it over before cutting into four and eating.*

In a wok, combine the palm sugar, fish sauce and tamarind and simmer until the sugar has dissolved. Do not boil. Skim the liquid, then check the taste – it should be sweet and sour. Adjust with palm sugar, fish sauce or tamarind.

Take out the sauce and clean the wok. Heat the vegetable oil and fry the eggs for 4–5 minutes until blistered and light brown. Remove and drain.

To serve, cut the eggs into quarters and place in a bowl. In a separate bowl, combine the coriander and fried garnish. Pour the palm sugar sauce over the eggs and serve scattered with the garnish.

# TTEOKBOKKI
# (KOREAN RICE CAKES WITH SPICY PORK)

**SERVES 2**

500g tteok (long Korean
rice cakes)

2 tablespoons vegetable oil

½ onion, finely diced

1 carrot, peeled and
finely diced

200g minced pork

5 small spring onions,
finely sliced

1 fresh green chilli, finely sliced

*For the sauce*

2 tablespoons doenjang
(fermented soya bean paste)

2 tablespoons gochujang
(Korean chilli paste)

1 tablespoon apple
cider vinegar

1 tablespoon good-quality
sesame oil

1 teaspoon minced garlic

200ml lemonade

*To garnish*

2 spring onions, finely chopped

1 fresh green chilli, finely sliced

1 tablespoon sesame seeds

*The very first time I ate these Korean rice cakes was not in Korea, but in a restaurant called Ssäm in New York and I was smitten. These rice cakes are chewy, but that's what I like – the texture. The sauce is not classic, but is instead my own idea – it's a Korean bolognese and when the crew ate it they said* mashisoyo, *which means 'delicious'. Actually what it means is 'taste exists', but it also means delicious!*

If the rice cakes are fresh, then skip this step, otherwise, if they are hard, soak them in enough warm water to cover for 30 minutes, then drain but keep the soaking liquid.

Heat 1 tablespoon of the vegetable oil in a large frying pan over a medium heat and add the rice cakes. Fry for 2–3 minutes, turning occasionally, until the sides start to colour and become golden and crispy. Remove the rice cakes from the pan and set to one side.

Put the remaining vegetable oil into the frying pan and heat over a high heat. Add the onion, carrot and minced pork to the pan, flatten everything down to create nice crispy bits when it browns at the bottom, and leave for 2–3 minutes until cooked through. Add the spring onions and chilli and cook for a further 2–3 minutes.

Mix together all the ingredients for the sauce in a small bowl, then add it to the pan and mix everything together. Boil for 2 minutes until the liquid reduces and becomes a little sticky, constantly keeping everything moving.

When the sauce thickens, add 2–3 tablespoons of the soaking liquid from the rice cakes (or water) to loosen. Add the rice cakes to the pan, and reheat them in the sauce.

Combine the spring onions, green chilli and sesame seeds.

Serve the rice cake mix immediately with the garnish sprinkled over the top.

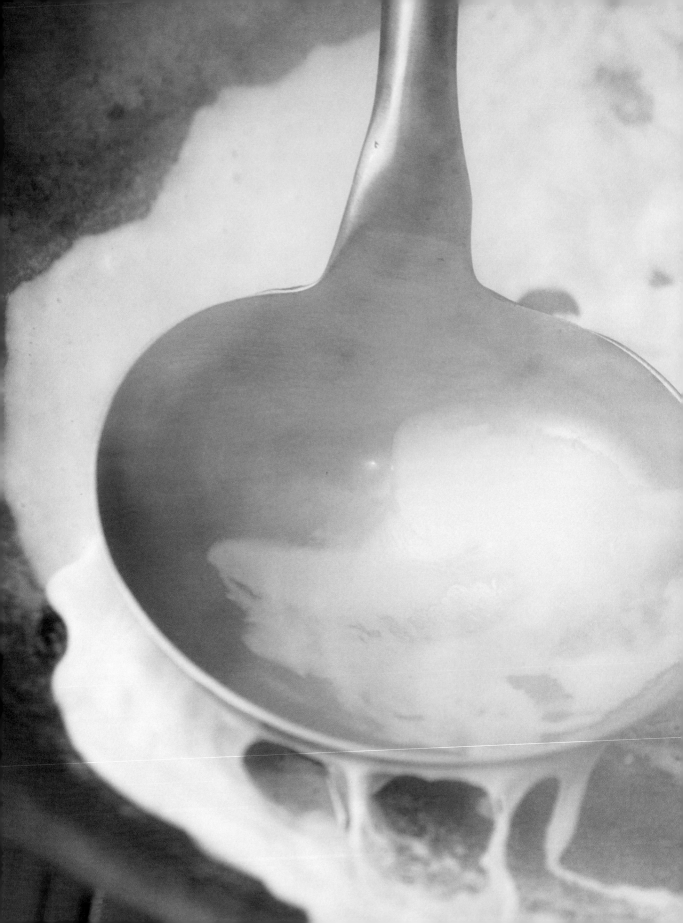

# CURRIES & SOUPS

Never judge a simple soup or a simmering curry by its appearance. Rivers run deep and all these broths, stews and curries have a different personality, wear their own fragrance and seduce with their complexity. So many people I meet on my travels tell me their secret – one lady said you must fry the paste for ten minutes, another swore it should be fifteen. In Malaysia the curry pastes are always blended, while in Thailand they pound them. Everyone has their own way.

# PORK RED CURRY WITH BAMBOO

........................................................

**SERVES 6–8**

100ml vegetable oil

1kg pork leg (skin and fat attached), cut into 8 pieces

100ml fish sauce

2 x 400ml tins coconut milk

3 tablespoons red curry paste (bought or see page 138)

2 tablespoons palm sugar

6 lemongrass stalks

10 double lime leaves

2 thumb-sized pieces of fresh galangal, chopped

200g large bamboo shoots

2 fresh red chillies, sliced

2 handfuls of fresh coriander

100g beansprouts

a handful of crispy fried onions, to serve

*You can buy the red curry paste or make it yourself and, if you do make it, then make a whole batch, which is more than you need for the recipe below. Store the extra in the freezer. Use big hunks of pork, then cut them up afterwards and add them back to the sauce. That way you get lovely moist pieces rather than little bits of dried pork.*

........................................................

In a large heavy pan, heat the vegetable oil and seal the pork hunks really well so they have lots and lots of colour on all sides. Don't let the skin get stuck – if it will not come away from the pan, don't force it, it will release itself. Now add half the fish sauce and tip the whole lot into a bowl whilst you make the sauce.

Heat a wok, add the creamy top layer of the coconut milk from the tins and bring to the boil. When it splits, add the curry paste and stir well. Reduce the heat and cook the paste for 3 minutes or so until fragrant. Now add the palm sugar and cook for a minute so it becomes rich and dark and red. Next, drop in all the aromatics – the lemongrass, lime leaves and galangal – and give a good stir to release their oils.

Pour the pork and all the liquid that sits in with it into the paste and give it a good stir so the pork is all coated. Add the remaining coconut milk and bring to the boil.

Add 300ml water, reduce the heat to a simmer and drop in the bamboo shoots. Cook slowly for 40 minutes, topping up with water occasionally and giving it the odd stir so it doesn't stick, but be gentle.

Take the pork and slice into four, then pop back into the sauce and season with the remaining fish sauce if needed.

Mix the sliced chilli with the coriander and the beansprouts, top the curry with this garnish and the crispy fried onions and serve with rice.

# RED CURRY PASTE

MAKES ENOUGH FOR
3–4 CURRIES

50g medium dried red chillies

1 teaspoon white peppercorns

½ teaspoon coriander seeds

½ teaspoon cumin seeds

2 whole cloves

½ teaspoon mace blade

1 thumb-sized piece of fresh
galangal, roughly chopped

1 lemongrass stalk, outer
leaves removed and inner
leaves roughly chopped

3 fresh red chillies, de-seeded
and roughly chopped

3 garlic cloves, peeled

3 small Thai shallots, chopped

a handful of fresh coriander
root, soaked and washed

finely grated zest of 1 lime

1 teaspoon salt

25g shrimp paste, toasted
(see Tip)

6 lime leaves

2 tablespoons vegetable oil

*Buy good-quality dried red chillies that are crisp and that you snap open so the seeds fall out. If you add the seeds, not only will the paste and the curry be ferociously hot, but they will also be bitter.*

Ideally, I would use a mortar and pestle for this, but a good strong food processor works well, too.

Snap the stalk end from the dried red chillies and shake out the seeds. Put the dried chillies into a bowl and cover with hot water. Leave for about 20 minutes until they have plumped up, then drain but keep them wet.

Heat a small dry frying pan over a medium heat until hot, then add the peppercorns, both lots of seeds, the cloves and mace blade and dry-fry, stirring regularly, until nicely toasted, about 2 minutes.

Tip the toasted spices into a mortar and pestle or food processor and pound or blend to a fine powder. Add the galangal and lemongrass and pound or blend to a paste. Add all the remaining ingredients, including the soaked chillies, and pound or blend to a paste.

Tip
To toast shrimp paste, wrap it in foil, then place it in a hot dry frying pan and cook for 2 minutes. Turn it over, turn the heat off and leave for a further 2 minutes. The paste will puff up and be toasted and fragrant, but less pungent.

# SPICY PRAWNS AND SCALLOPS WITH PUMPKIN

**SERVES 8**

1 x 200g packet of
    creamed coconut

4 tablespoons red curry paste
    (bought or see opposite)

2 tablespoons palm sugar

1 tablespoon fish sauce

200g pumpkin or butternut
    squash flesh

2 x 400ml tins coconut milk

200g fresh large raw prawns,
    peeled and deveined,
    tails left on

8 large fresh scallops

a bunch of Thai basil or
    ordinary basil, leaves picked

*This is simple, quick and delicious. The pumpkin curry can be made the night before and then reheated, with the prawns and scallops added at the last minute. Serve with big bowls of steaming rice. This is just as good served as a pasta sauce – use fettuccine, it's ace.*

Set a wok or large heavy-based pan over a low heat. Put all but 2 tablespoons of the creamed coconut into the wok, stirring constantly until it all melts and starts to split into an oily mess. Add the curry paste, increase the heat and fry, stirring constantly. After 5 minutes the paste should be fragrant and sizzling in oil.

Stir in the rest of the creamed coconut, add the palm sugar and bring up to a simmer, then add the fish sauce. Add the pumpkin or squash and cook for 1 minute. Now add the coconut milk and simmer for about 10 minutes until the pumpkin is soft. At this stage the curry can be left and reheated. Otherwise, add the prawns and bring to the boil, then cook for 2 minutes – the prawns should turn red and go crunchy. Add the scallops and cook for a further 3 minutes.

Pour the curry into a large serving dish or individual bowls and garnish with the basil leaves. The curry should be sweet and creamy.

# CHOO CHEE FISH

**SERVES 4–6**

400ml tin coconut milk

20g red curry paste (bought or see page 138)

2 tablespoons palm sugar

2 tablespoons fish sauce

12 lime leaves, finely shredded

750g monkfish, cod or similar white fish fillets (or even large fresh raw prawns with shell on) or a mixture

fresh lime juice, to taste

½ bunch of fresh Thai basil, leaves picked

*The technique shown here for making a curry paste is the foundation for many of the Thai curries in this book.*

*I used to make this dish at Mezzo years ago and as for its origin I could research it, I guess, but I feel I need to be honest and say it is just one of those recipes that happened along the way. I also sort of like the name, it reminds me of Chitty Chitty Bang Bang and the song sung in the square by the old German man to his young mistress. I think he called her 'choochy face'!*

Warm the creamy top layer of the coconut milk in a wok over a medium heat until it boils gently, then cook for 6–8 minutes, stirring occasionally, until it splits into oil and solids but is still white. Add the red curry paste and stir to dissolve the paste into the coconut, cooking for a further 3 minutes or so.

Add the rest of the coconut milk, palm sugar, fish sauce and half the shredded lime leaves and stir. Cook for 8–10 minutes, stirring until the curry is reduced and thickened. Taste and adjust the seasoning with extra fish sauce, palm sugar or curry paste, if necessary. It should have plenty of flavour.

Now add the fish or prawns or even both, return to a simmer and cook for 5 minutes until the fish is cooked.

Remove from the heat, stir in the rest of the lime leaves and some lime juice to taste and serve, with basil leaves scattered across the top. Serve on noodles.

*Step-by-step pictures on pages 142–143*

ADD PALM SUGAR AND COOK UNTIL DONE

# BUTTERNUT SQUASH RED CURRY WITH TOFU

**SERVES 4–6**

1 medium butternut squash

300g firm tofu

vegetable oil, for frying

150g red curry paste (bought or see page 138)

125g creamed coconut

2 x 400ml tins coconut milk

40g palm sugar

4 lemongrass stalks, bruised

12 lime leaves, torn

4 thumb-sized pieces of galangal, roughly chopped

1 tablespoon fish sauce (or add a vegetarian fish sauce substitute or 1 teaspoon salt)

*To garnish*

Fried Garnish (see page 204)

1 fresh red chilli, sliced (optional)

*The red curry, in my opinion, is the richest and most satisfying to make of all the curries. It is the flavour of Thailand in one addictive sauce. The process of cooking out the paste, then adding the palm sugar and cooking again until the paste becomes baked terracotta-red, rich, fragrant and the consistency of jam, is paramount for a really red curry.*

Peel and de-seed the butternut squash, then cut into large hunks the size of golf balls. Cut the tofu into similar-sized pieces. Set both to one side.

Heat a little vegetable oil in a medium saucepan, then add the curry paste and cook for a minute or so. Add the creamed coconut and the creamy layer from the top of the tins of coconut milk and cook over a medium heat for 5–6 minutes – it will start to colour and smell of roasted coconut, but watch that it doesn't burn.

Now add the palm sugar, reduce the heat and cook gently for about 5–10 minutes, stirring until it is rich red in colour and no longer smells raw. The oil will separate from the mixture and then gradually start to come back together as the mixture thickens and darkens. Be careful not to let it burn.

Add the squash pieces and stir well so that the paste coats them all, cook for a couple of minutes, then pour in the coconut milk and 200ml water and bring to the boil. Drop in the lemongrass, lime leaves and galangal, add half the fish sauce, then reduce the heat and simmer gently, uncovered, for 10–12 minutes. Stir in the tofu and simmer gently for a further 10 minutes.

To finish, season with extra palm sugar if it's too spicy, or the remaining fish sauce if it's a little bland. The sauce should taste sweet, hot and just slightly salty.

Dress with some fried garnish and the sliced chilli and serve immediately.

# THAI GREEN CHICKEN CURRY

.........................................................

**FEEDS 8 PEOPLE AS PART OF
A BIGGER SPREAD SERVED
WITH LOTS OF RICE**

2 x 400ml tins coconut milk

2 teaspoons vegetable oil

2 tablespoons green curry
  paste (bought or
  see opposite)

40g palm sugar

80ml fish sauce

50g pea aubergines, picked

50g apple aubergines,
  quartered

20g lime leaves

300g skinless, boneless chicken
  meat, diced

a small bunch of fresh Thai
  basil, leaves picked

3 long fresh red chillies,
  sliced lengthways

*I am a big fan of the green curry because the fact that it uses whole fresh green chillies with the seeds in means it is the spiciest of the coconut milk curries. Having recently made this on my last trip to Bangkok, and having served it to locals, I have tweaked this recipe, which has sat in my repertoire for over 25 years. It will be spicy hot, green and delicious. Serve with lots of rice.*

*I am including the recipe for green curry paste in full opposite, although you can buy green curry paste. If you do, spruce it up with lime zest, lemongrass and coriander roots, as well as shallots and garlic, so the store-bought paste becomes fresher and more vibrant.*

.........................................................

I like to cook this curry in a wok as I think it is easier, but a large, heavy-based pot will do.

Heat the wok until warm, then drop in the creamy top layer of the coconut milk tins. Turn the heat to medium and let the cream boil, then add the vegetable oil. When the cream has boiled and split into oil and solid, add the curry paste (adding more if you would like it hotter!). Stir and cook gently for a good 10 minutes until fragrant and smelling of cooked onions. As it cooks, add a little spoonful of the coconut milk or water if it looks a little dry.

Add the palm sugar and fish sauce and stir well until melted, then add the aubergines and lime leaves, stir and cook for 5 minutes to soften the vegetables. Add the remaining coconut milk and bring to the boil, then reduce to a simmer, add the chicken and simmer gently for 5 minutes. Remove from the heat and leave to infuse for about 10 minutes. The flavour should be hot and salty, so add a little more fish sauce and sugar if needed.

Garnish with Thai basil leaves and sliced red chilli and serve immediately.

# GREEN CURRY PASTE

........................................................

**MAKES ENOUGH FOR
3–4 CURRIES**

*With all curry pastes, should you wish to store the paste, you are best to cook it first and then store (a fresh uncooked paste will only keep for a day or so in the fridge). Once cooked, leave the paste to cool, then store in sealed jars (enough for a curry each) in the freezer.*

........................................................

1 teaspoon coriander seeds

1 teaspoon cumin seeds

1 teaspoon white peppercorns

finely grated zest of 1 lime

1 teaspoon coarse salt

5–6 fresh coriander roots, soaked and washed

3 lemongrass stalks, shredded

a small knob of fresh turmeric, peeled

1 thumb-sized piece of galangal, chopped

6 long fresh green chillies, de-seeded and chopped

5 fresh scud or bird's eye chillies, chopped

50g shrimp paste, toasted (see Tip on page 138)

6 small Thai shallots, roughly chopped

1 bulb of garlic, cloves peeled

Heat a small, dry frying pan until hot, then add the coriander seeds, cumin seeds and peppercorns. Turn off the heat and let the spices toast in the hot pan for a few minutes until fragrant, tossing every minute or so to keep them moving. Leave to cool, then grind to a powder using a mortar and pestle.

Using a mortar and pestle, pound the lime zest, salt and coriander roots together, then add the lemongrass and pound to a paste (you have to do it in this order, otherwise the paste will be stringy). Stir in the toasted ground spices. Next add the turmeric, galangal and chopped chillies and pound well. Now add the shrimp paste and pound it well, then finally add the shallots and garlic as these both contain a lot of water and will make the paste wet.

If you prefer to use a food processor, then you are best to buy a ready-made paste and add the pounded lime zest, coriander roots and lemongrass, then pound in the chopped shallots and garlic to form a paste.

# KOREAN ARMY STEW

. . . . . . . . . . . . . . . . . . . . . . . . . . . . . . . . . . . . . . . . . . .

**THIS IS A DISH TO BE SHARED, ENOUGH FOR 2–4**

200g pack of Korean instant noodles (or just use any instant noodles)

150g spam, cut into 5cm squares

5 hot dogs, cut into 5cm slices (or if you can get the little Korean ones with cut ends, even better)

35g straw mushrooms

200g firm tofu

100g kimchi, roughly chopped (bought or see page 244), plus some kimchi juice

1 tablespoon gochujang (Korean chilli paste)

2 garlic cloves, finely chopped

5 spring onions, cut into 5cm lengths

white pepper, to taste

3 slices of processed cheese

*This is a real surprise, and I mean surprise – it is addictive like few things I have eaten and yes, it is made up of the most disparate of parts. Give it a go – it's bloody great student food and a real talking point at a dinner party. You really do have to eat it to believe its brilliance!*

*My first visit to Korea was a real culture shock; there are no two ways about it. The Koreans are very extraordinary people, with food that few people know anything about. This stew was born out of a time when there was nothing, when the Korean war was nearly over and the only meat came from tins smuggled out of American army bases. Spam is still held in very high regard in Korea and now I love it too.*

. . . . . . . . . . . . . . . . . . . . . . . . . . . . . . . . . . . . . . . . . . .

I use a deep frying pan for this, as I think it works best, but a casserole dish that can sit on the stove will do.

Put the instant noodles in the bottom of the pan, then layer the other ingredients on top – the spam, hot dogs, mushrooms, tofu, chopped kimchi (plus some kimchi juice) and all the remaining ingredients, except the cheese, seasoning with some white pepper as you go. Cover with water, then bring to a simmer and cook gently until the noodles are soft and the meat is hot, about 5 minutes.

Turn off the heat and place the cheese slices on top, let them melt and then serve.

*Step-by-step pictures on pages 150–151*

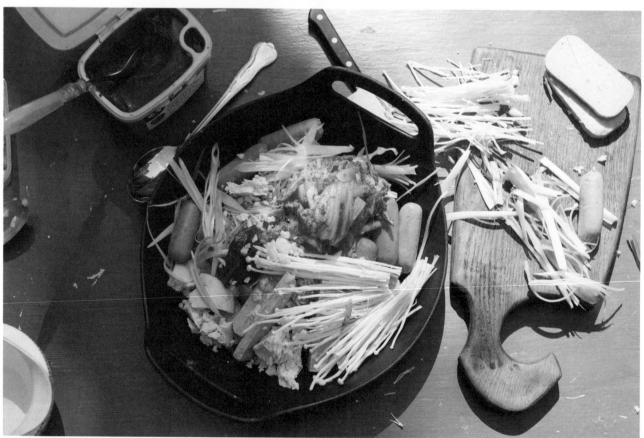

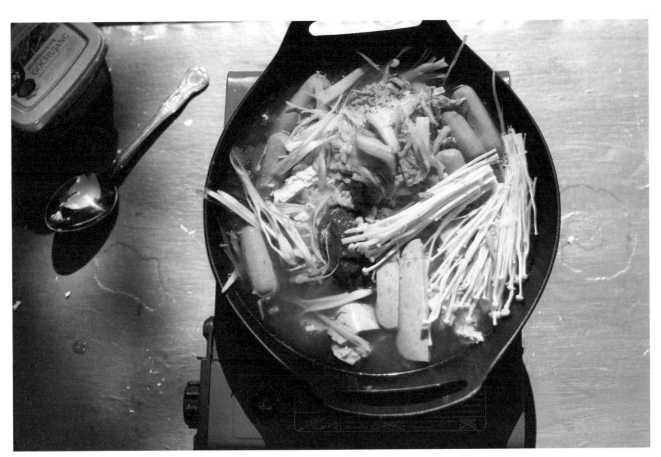

# BEEF RENDANG

## FEEDS ABOUT 8–10

40g coriander seeds

1 teaspoon cumin seeds

1 teaspoon ground turmeric

2 lemongrass stalks, shredded

1 teaspoon coarse salt

50ml vegetable oil

3 large onions, finely chopped

6 garlic cloves, grated

6 large long fresh red
chillies, chopped

3 thumb-sized pieces of
fresh root ginger, peeled
and grated

1.5kg stewing beef (I think shin
is the very best), cut into
2.5cm squares

6 bay leaves

2 x 400ml tins coconut milk

100g creamed coconut

500ml hot beef stock

*Rendang, rendang everywhere! I love this recipe and have been cooking variations and adaptations of it for over two decades. There are many versions of rendang and many arguments over whose is best. Some say it originated in Malaysia, some say in Indonesia, others say Singapore; wherever it first came from I don't mind, but I am eternally grateful. Oh, and remember to freeze what's not eaten, if that is at all possible. This recipe appeared in my last book,* My Kind of Food, *but it was so popular that I am also including it in this book.*

Put the coriander and cumin seeds and the turmeric into a dry frying pan and toast gently for 2 minutes until nutty and fragrant. Grind to a fine powder using a mortar and pestle, then add the shredded lemongrass and the salt and pound until it forms a paste and is as smooth as possible.

In a wok or large pan, heat the vegetable oil. Drop in the onions and cook slowly and gently for a few minutes, then add the garlic, chillies, ginger and spice paste and cook gently until the onions are softened and your kitchen starts to smell like Asia. Add 125ml water and cook for a further 5 minutes, stirring always. Now add the meat and bay leaves and increase the heat. Stir the meat around so it is coated in the spice mix but be careful not to burn it.

Cook for a few minutes until the meat has coloured a little.

Add the coconut milk and creamed coconut, bring to the boil, then add the hot stock. Turn the heat to medium. Now this will cook for a good 2 hours. Stir often, scraping the bottom of the wok with a wooden spoon so the paste doesn't stick. Over the next hour or so the liquid will simmer and reduce to become a thick sauce. It will need to be stirred constantly for the last 5–10 minutes or so, so that it doesn't stick.

This is a dry curry: all the sweet coconut and spices should end up wrapped around the tender chunks of meat and there should be very little liquid. Keep cooking it if it's not thick enough.

Serve with Roti Jala (see opposite).

# ROTI JALA

**MAKES ABOUT 6**

150g plain flour

1 egg

100ml coconut milk

pinch of salt

drop of yellow food colouring
(not necessary, but some
people add this!)

*This recipe uses a roti jala maker, a super-cheap piece of equipment you can buy online. If you don't have one, a plastic squeezy bottle works too.*

Put all the ingredients into a large jug, along with 250ml water, and whisk together until smooth, making sure you get out all lumps – it's just like making a pancake batter. Pour the batter through a strainer or sieve.

Now heat a large, non-stick frying pan until hot, then pour some of the batter into a roti jala maker and start swirling the batter in a circular motion into the frying pan. You have to be quick, and once you have enough swirls to cover the pan, quickly pop the roti jala maker to one side and flip the roti jala so it cooks on the other side. It should only take a minute to cook on each side.

Once cooked, slide onto a plate, fold the sides in and roll into a log shape. Keep warm. Continue until you have used up all your batter.

Serve with your Beef Rendang (see opposite).

# SOUR YELLOW CURRY OF VEGETABLES

**SERVES 4–6**

*For the curry paste*
30g dried shrimps, soaked
    (see Tip)
200g long fresh yellow
    chillies, chopped
6 small Thai shallots, chopped
3 garlic cloves, chopped
50g fresh galangal, chopped
2 teaspoons salt
2 teaspoons shrimp paste,
    toasted (see Tip on
    page 138)
20g fresh turmeric, peeled
    and chopped
4 teaspoons vegetable oil
    (if you are using a food
    processor)

*For the curry*
700ml vegetable stock or water
pinch of salt
2 teaspoons caster sugar
4 tablespoons concentrated
    cooking tamarind, plus extra
    to serve
3 Chinese cabbage leaves,
    cut in half
500g potatoes, cut into chunks
500g pumpkin or butternut
    squash, peeled, de-seeded
    and cut into chunks
500g sweet potatoes, cut
    into chunks
2 fresh yellow chillies, split
100g sugar snap peas
100g snake (yard long) beans,
    cut on an angle
2 tablespoons vegetable oil
2 tablespoons fish sauce, or
    to taste
100g beansprouts

*This sour curry is properly sour, using just tamarind for the sharpness. There is no coconut here, which points to a curry from the north of Thailand, where coconuts just don't happen. All the vegetables are soft and sweet and the sauce is sour and spicy. Getting your hands on yellow chillies can be tricky, so sometimes a little extra turmeric is helpful for colour.*

First make the curry paste. You can either make the paste using a mortar and pestle or use a food processor that chops properly and fast. Either pound or blend all the ingredients together to make a paste.

To make the curry, in a medium saucepan combine the stock, salt, sugar and tamarind, then bring to the boil. Drop the cabbage, potato, pumpkin and sweet potato into the boiling liquid, along with the yellow chillies, then simmer for 20 minutes. Add the sugar snap peas and beans for the last 5 minutes and cook all the vegetables until just soft.

Remove the vegetables and chillies to a plate using a slotted spoon and put to one side. Reserve the stock.

Heat the vegetable oil in a separate saucepan, add 60g of the yellow curry paste and fry over a medium heat for 5–6 minutes. Stir in the reserved stock from the vegetables and season with the fish sauce.

To finish, return the vegetables to the stock mixture, bring back to the boil to warm through, then add a little extra tamarind water and/or fish sauce to make the curry more sour or salty.

Put the beansprouts into a large bowl and pour the vegetable curry over.

Serve in little bowls alongside rice or rice noodles.

Tip
Soak the dried shrimps in warm water for 10 minutes until bloated, then drain. They are now ready to use.

# JUNGLE CURRY OF FISH

. . . . . . . . . . . . . . . . . . . . . . . . . . . . . . . .

**ENOUGH FOR 4–6**

*For the curry paste*
2 teaspoons white peppercorns
50g salt
8 fresh green chillies, half de-
    seeded and half seeds left in
10 small Thai shallots, chopped
10 garlic cloves, chopped
3 lemongrass stalks, outer
    leaves removed and inner
    leaves finely sliced
2 large thumb-sized pieces of
    fresh galangal, sliced
10 fresh coriander roots,
    soaked and washed
zest of 2 limes
50g krachai (fingerroot/lesser
    galangal), peeled and sliced
30g shrimp paste, toasted (see
    Tip on page 138)

*For the curry*
50ml vegetable oil
4 teaspoons fish sauce
20g palm sugar
100ml Mekhong whisky or
    Chinese (Shaoxing) rice wine
6 lime leaves, torn
100g krachai (fingerroot/lesser
    galangal), scraped and cut
    into julienne
50g fresh or tinned bamboo
    shoots, cut into pieces
2 litres chicken stock
2 handfuls of fresh clams
12 small fresh prawns, shell on
6 small green aubergines, cut
    into quarters
6 snake (yard long) beans, cut
    into pieces
300g snapper or bream fillets
a bunch of fresh Thai basil,
    leaves picked

*The further north you go in Thailand, the closer you come to the borders of Laos and Burma and the food changes dramatically. Gone are the sweet coconut curries of the south and instead they become drier and spicier, richer and more herbaceous. This recipe is great with river fish like carp, or even barramundi, but I have adapted it a little so it's a bit more user-friendly. Traditionally the paste is made by pounding all the ingredients in a mortar and pestle, but you can blend them once you have ground your spices.*

. . . . . . . . . . . . . . . . . . . . . . . . . . . . . . . . . . . . . . . . . . . . .

Using a mortar and pestle, make the curry paste by grinding the peppercorns and salt to a powder. Add to a food processor with all the remaining ingredients and blend quickly to make a curry paste, adding no liquid.

In a wok, heat the vegetable oil over a high heat. Add 2 tablespoons of the curry paste and stir it for a few minutes until fragrant, then reduce the heat and cook gently for 5 minutes. Add the fish sauce and palm sugar and turn up the heat. Now add the booze and stir well to cook off the alcohol, then continue to fry for another minute. Add the lime leaves, krachai and bamboo shoots, then add the stock and bring to the boil. Cook at a gentle simmer for 10 minutes.

Add the cleaned clams and prawns and cook for a few minutes until the clams open, then add the aubergines, snake beans and fish and cook for a further 3–5 minutes. Discard any clams that remain closed.

Serve with the basil scattered over the top.

# HANGOVER SOUP WITH MUNG BEAN SPROUTS AND SEAWEED

## FOR ABOUT 2 PEOPLE

2 handfuls of fresh mung
   bean sprouts

500ml vegetable stock

3 garlic cloves, grated

2 small fresh green hot chillies,
   finely sliced, plus extra
   to serve

3 small spring onions, finely
   sliced, plus extra to serve

*To serve*

2 eggs

seaweed sheets (or use 1 nori
   sheet, cut into 6)

*In Korea, food of all types is said to be good for you. I mean everything! This is a real dish – I have sat and eaten it next to a couple who were at the hangover soup stall early in the morning because they'd had a big night out and needed a pick-me-up. I have no recipe for this, but simply watched the stallholder make it. It is delicious, though I am yet to test it out on a hangover.*

Preheat a couple of large bowls and drop in the mung bean sprouts. Heat the stock in a pan and when it is simmering, add the garlic, chillies and spring onions.

Crack the eggs into two ramekins or small cocottes and steam in a water bath on the hob for 4–5 minutes or until the eggs are cooked but the yolks still soft.

Pour the soup over the bean sprouts and serve each portion with seaweed sheets and a steamed egg on the side, plus extra chilli and spring onion to sprinkle over.

# MASSAMAN CHICKEN AND PRAWN CURRY

**FEEDS 8–10**

*For the paste*
20g white peppercorns
2 lemongrass stalks, outer
    leaves removed and inner
    leaves shredded
pared zest of 1 lime, chopped
50g shrimp paste, toasted
    (see Tip on page 138)
20g dried shrimps, soaked
    (see Tip on page 154)
6 large fresh red chillies, de-
    seeded and chopped
5 fingers of krachai (fingerroot/
    lesser galangal), peeled
1 thumb-sized piece of fresh
    galangal, chopped
4 small Thai shallots, sliced
6 garlic cloves, chopped
1 teaspoon salt

*For the curry*
2 x 400ml tins coconut milk
50ml vegetable oil
30g palm sugar
40ml fish sauce
4 tablespoons concentrated
    cooking tamarind
1 pineapple, peeled, cored and
    chopped into large pieces
10 lime leaves, torn
4 large fresh red chillies, split
    down the centre
2 lemongrass stalks, outer
    leaves removed and cut into
    3cm pieces
6 skinless, boneless chicken
    thighs, each cut into 3 pieces
about 20 large fresh raw
    prawns, peeled and deveined

*Massaman curries are curries derived from the Muslims who travelled the known world, moving and trading spices all over Asia. It is a complex but beautiful Thai curry. The recipe is for eight to ten, but even if there are only four of you, I bet you finish the whole bloody lot!*

I like to make this paste using a mortar and pestle, but please do it in the order of the ingredients so that it becomes smooth, beginning with the peppercorns and grinding to a powder, then adding two ingredients at a time and pounding them to a paste before adding the next two. Continue in this way until all the ingredients have been added and pounded. Alternatively, you can put all the ingredients in a food processor and blend together to form a paste. Add some salt to the paste, if necessary.

In a wok, gently melt the top layer of the coconut milk from the tins, add the vegetable oil and cook until they split, stirring to stop the cream burning. Add 100g of the curry paste and fry until fragrant, then push the paste to one side, drop in the palm sugar and let it melt. Add the fish sauce and stir the paste into it, then add the tamarind and cook until it becomes a dark colour, stirring gently. Add the remaining coconut milk and the pineapple, then bring to the boil.

Put the lime leaves, chillies and lemongrass into the wok, then reduce the heat and cook gently for 20 minutes. Now drop in the chicken pieces, bring back to the boil and cook for 3 minutes, then add the prawns, bring back to the boil once again and cook for a further 3 minutes or until the chicken is cooked and the prawns have taken on their wonderful pink colour.

Remove from the heat and leave for 5 minutes before serving with noodles or rice. The curry should be sour and sweet and quite spicy.

# SPICED MONKFISH BROTH WITH LEMONGRASS AND GINGER

......................................................................

**FEEDS 4**

1 litre chicken stock

3 lemongrass stalks, crushed

4 fresh coriander roots, soaked and washed, then crushed

1 large thumb-sized piece of fresh root ginger, peeled and cut into matchsticks

12 small tomatoes, cut in half

6 lime leaves, torn

juice of 1 lime, plus extra to serve

4 teaspoons concentrated cooking tamarind

3 fresh red chillies, split lengthways and de-seeded

a little vegetable oil, for frying

200g monkfish fillet, diced

a small bunch of fresh Thai basil, leaves picked

2 tablespoons fish sauce, or to taste

palm sugar, to taste

fresh coriander, leaves picked, to garnish

*Monkfish lends itself to many a classic soup or broth because it holds up well and stays firm. Soups generally are a meal in Asia and a big bowlful is served with some rice on the side to eat with it; this recipe is no exception. Add noodles if you like, and serve with extra chopped chilli or nam prik (see page 81), the classic condiment of fish sauce and chopped chillies with seeds in, to help the spice along.*

......................................................................

In a large pan, bring the stock and 500ml water to the boil, then add the lemongrass, coriander root, ginger, tomatoes, lime leaves, lime juice, tamarind and red chillies. Reduce the heat and simmer very gently for 15 minutes. Remove from the heat.

Heat a little vegetable oil in a wok, then add the monkfish and stir-fry over a high heat for a good 3 minutes or so until cooked. Transfer the monkfish to a large serving bowl, add the Thai basil to the soup, season to taste with the fish sauce and palm sugar, then pour the soup over the monkfish.

Garnish with coriander leaves and a squeeze of extra lime juice to taste.

# MALAY PINEAPPLE CURRY WITH COCONUT RICE

...........................................................

**SERVES 4–6**

5cm piece of fresh root
    ginger, peeled

½ bulb of garlic, cloves peeled

25g meat curry powder or
    fish curry powder
    (preferably Malaysian)

8 tablespoons vegetable oil

5 stems of fresh curry leaves

1 cinnamon stick

3 star anise

3 cardamom pods

4 whole cloves

6 banana shallots, thinly
    sliced lengthways (or 1 large
    onion, diced)

1 tablespoon concentrated
    cooking tamarind

1 large pineapple, peeled,
    cored and cut into chunks

1 tablespoon palm sugar

400ml tin coconut milk

2 tablespoons kerisik (see Tip)

salt or fish sauce, to taste

Coconut Rice (see opposite),
    to serve

*Wherever I go I always try and have a least one cooking lesson somewhere and this little gem was taught to me by a lady called Naslema, overlooking a market in Penang. It was 35°C outside and the result was a cooling and very satisfying, delicious, toasty curry. She also taught me how to make kerisik, which is cooked desiccated coconut pounded into a paste – this is the secret seasoning for this curry, so please make the extra effort, it's well worth it.*

.........................................................................

Either pound the ginger and garlic together until fine using a mortar and pestle or grate them both.

Make a curry paste by adding 150ml water to the curry powder – the paste should be a bit watery.

Heat the vegetable oil in a wok or saucepan over a medium heat and when it is slightly smoky, drop in the curry leaves. Add in the four sibling spices (cinnamon stick, star anise, cardamoms and cloves) and fry for 10 seconds. Now add the shallots and the ginger and garlic paste and stir-fry until slightly brown. Then stir in the curry powder paste. This is the most important part of making the curry, so ideally use a very low heat at this stage and wait until the oil separates from and bubbles all over the paste, about 4–5 minutes. Periodically scrape the bottom of the pan to remove the crust.

Add the tamarind, then the pineapple pieces and palm sugar. Stir in the creamy top layer of the tin of coconut milk. You may want to add a little more of the remaining thinner coconut milk to make the dish more saucy, but too much will make it less spicy. When the mixture starts boiling, add the kerisik, then reduce the heat to low and simmer for 10 minutes until the pineapple becomes translucent. Season with salt or fish sauce to taste, then serve with the Coconut Rice.

Tip
To make kerisik, roast some desiccated coconut in a dry frying pan, stirring constantly, until toasted and dark brown. Remove from the heat, tip into a mortar, then using the pestle pound the hot coconut until the oil comes out.

# COCONUT RICE

**SERVES 6**

300g long grain fragrant rice

2 teaspoons salt

100ml coconut milk

Wash the rice in cold water three times until the water runs clear, then drain well.

In a saucepan with a tight-fitting lid, put the rice, salt and coconut milk, along with 450ml water. Put the lid on the pan and bring the mix to the boil, then reduce the heat and cook for 5 minutes on a low simmer.

Turn off the heat but do not touch it, do not lift the lid! Leave for 20 minutes and it will be perfect and ready by absorption. Fluff up with a fork and serve.

# TOM KHA GAI

..........................................

SERVES 4–6

4 stalks of coriander with their roots, soaked and washed

200ml chicken stock

2 x 400ml tins coconut milk

2 lemongrass stalks, cut and bruised

8 thick slices of galangal

10 lime leaves, torn

4 tablespoons concentrated cooking tamarind

4 small fresh green chillies, crushed in a mortar

4 tablespoons fish sauce

2 skinless, boneless chicken breasts, sliced lengthways

juice of 2 limes

lots of fresh coriander and Thai basil leaves, to garnish

*There are two very classic and well-known soups in Thailand: Tom Yum, Hot and Sour Soup, and Tom Kha, Hot and Sour Soup with coconut. This one has the addition of chicken, which is Gai, so Tom Kha Gai. In the south of Thailand coconuts grow in abundance, and the milk extracted from their flesh is used for everything. This soup can hold a lot of spice – the number of chillies indicates that – because of the sweetness that is generated when using coconut.*

..........................................

Separate the coriander leaves from the stems, then crush the roots and stems. Put to one side.

In a large pot, combine the stock, coconut milk, lemongrass, galangal and coriander stalks and bring to the boil, then reduce the heat and simmer for 4 minutes.

Add the lime leaves, tamarind and chillies, then return to the boil and add the fish sauce. Taste it and it should be sweet, sour, salty and hot, but play with the seasoning if you feel you need to. Drop in the chicken slices and cook for 2 minutes.

Serve in big bowls with a good squirt of lime juice in the bottom of each one and pour the soup over it along with lots of herbs to garnish.

# WHOLE QUAILS IN CURRY ON THE ROAD IN MALACCA

**SERVES 4**

*For the curry paste*

100g fresh root ginger, peeled and grated

12 large dried red chillies

50g banana shallots, sliced

50g galangal, grated

1 lemongrass stalk, outer leaves removed and inner leaves shredded

2 garlic cloves, grated

2 teaspoons peeled and chopped fresh turmeric

2 tablespoons concentrated cooking tamarind

1 tablespoon belachan (shrimp paste), toasted (see Tip on page 138)

30g palm sugar

*For the quail curry*

100g ghee

1 teaspoon rice vinegar

2 large onions, sliced

4 whole quails, cleaned

3 stems of fresh curry leaves

50g plain flour

2 litres chicken stock

salt and freshly ground black pepper

Coconut Rice (see page 163), to serve

*Memories are wonderful. I could tell you a romantic story about the day I discovered this dish on the streets of Malacca in Malaysia. However, it was about two o'clock in the afternoon, it was 38°C and I was filming around Malaysia. My guide for the day was taking me through the markets and it was so hot. The stall where I found this had about ten different curries, and each pot had at least a hundred portions – it was the most impressive curry takeaway I have ever seen!*

Put 150ml water and the ginger into a bowl and leave to steep, then drain, reserving the ginger and soaking water separately.

Soak the dried chillies in hot water for 30 minutes until soft, then drain and chop into large pieces. Place in a food processor with the shallots, galangal, lemongrass, garlic, turmeric, ginger and tamarind and blend to combine. Add the toasted shrimp paste and palm sugar and blend again. Add some of the reserved ginger water and blend again to a smooth paste.

Heat a large saucepan over a low heat, add half the ghee, the vinegar and all the onions and fry for 30–40 minutes until they are soft and have loads of colour. Remove the onions to a plate and set aside.

Sprinkle a little salt and black pepper inside the quails, then place them in the large pan with the remaining ghee and cook over a high heat until they are golden on all sides. Now add the curry leaves and fry briefly with the quails, then remove the quails and leaves from the pan to a plate and set aside.

Add 100g of the curry paste to the pan and cook for 1–2 minutes, stirring, adding a splash or two of water if it starts to stick. Return the quails to the pan, sprinkle over the flour and stir, then add the stock and cooked onions. Scrape the bottom of the pan and make the whole thing smell amazing, then bring to a simmer and cook for 15–20 minutes, stirring once or twice.

Serve with Coconut Rice.

Tip
This can be made in advance and reheated later. Simply cool completely, store in the fridge for a couple of days, then reheat gently in a large pan until piping hot.

# MY LONG AND SHORT COMBINATION SOUP

. . . . . . . . . . . . . . . . . . . . . . . . . . . . . . . . . . . . . . . . . . . . . . . . .

**SERVES 6–8**

150–200g flat rice noodles

30 Wontons (see page 170)

bunch of spring onions, finely shredded, to garnish

*For the stock*

500ml fresh chicken stock

3 lemongrass stalks, bashed

1 large hand-sized piece of fresh root ginger, peeled and roughly chopped

3 garlic cloves, bashed

3 large thumb-sized pieces of galangal, roughly chopped

1 long fresh red chilli, split in half

12 lime leaves

2 star anise

a handful of fresh coriander root, soaked and washed, then smashed

2–3 tablespoons fish sauce, or to taste

*I am not going to tell you that this version of Long and Short Combination Soup has any origin except in my head. As a young boy in Australia, this was my go-to at the local and not-so-local Chinese – noodles and dumplings and a standard Chinese broth. When I opened Mezzo in 1995, I wanted those noodles and dumplings in soup, but didn't want to upset anyone in Chinatown, so I took the idea of using a Thai soup, noodles and some Chinese dumplings and pushed them all together. This is my Long and Short Combination Soup, circa 1995.*

. . . . . . . . . . . . . . . . . . . . . . . . . . . . . . . . . . . . . . . . . . . . . . . . .

Place all the stock ingredients together in a saucepan, add 1.5 litres water, bring gently to the boil, then simmer, uncovered, for 20 minutes.

Remove from the heat and leave to sit for an hour to infuse, then strain and discard the bits, reserving the stock.

Meanwhile, soak the noodles in warm water for 20 minutes, then drain.

When you are ready to serve, add the noodles to the reserved stock and heat until hot.

Divide the wontons among the bowls and pour in the stock and noodles. Garnish with the shredded spring onions and serve.

*Picture also on page 171*

# WONTONS

· · · · · · · · · · · · · · · · · · · · · · · · · · · · · · · · · · · · ·

**MAKES 30**

*Dumplings of any kind at any time of the day satisfy my hunger. These very simple ones make a quick meal on their own or can be added to a soup as here (see My Long and Short Combination Soup on page 168).*

30 wonton wrappers

*For the filling*

400g minced pork

45g fresh shiitake mushrooms, finely chopped

20g Chinese cabbage, finely shredded

1 spring onion, finely diced

1 teaspoon oyster sauce

1 teaspoon soy sauce

salt and freshly ground black pepper

Put all the ingredients for the filling into a mixing bowl and mix together well, seasoning with salt and black pepper.

Take a wonton wrapper, then with one hand make a loose fist. Place the wonton wrapper across the top of your fist so that it sits over your thumb and first finger with the centre covering the hole in the middle of your fist.

Put a heaped teaspoonful of the filling mixture into the centre of the wrapper and push it down a little into your fist so that the sides of the wrapper start to come up around it. Dip a finger of your other hand in water and dab around the edge of the filling, then use your fingers to pinch the wrapper tightly around the filling, leaving the top exposed. Tap the bottom of each dumpling on the work surface to flatten it, then put each one into lined steamer baskets as you go, continuing in the same way until you have made all the dumplings.

Bring a large pan of water to the boil, then put the filled steamer baskets on top and steam the dumplings for 5–6 minutes until the skins are translucent and the filling is cooked.

# CHINESE DUCK NOODLE SOUP

**FEEDS 4**

1 Chinese roast duck carcass

2 carrots, chopped

1 leek, trimmed, washed and chopped

1 onion, roughly chopped

2 celery sticks, roughly chopped

100g fresh root ginger, peeled and sliced

5 star anise

10 black peppercorns

2 tablespoons fish sauce

3 tablespoons good-quality toasted sesame oil

a large bunch of fresh coriander with roots (leaves and roots separated)

1kg pre-cooked egg noodles

4 spring onions, thinly sliced

1 fresh red chilli, cut into julienne

*The roasted bones of any poultry make wonderful stock, but a Chinese roast duck stock is another thing altogether. Think of the delicious smells that hit you when you first walk into a Chinese restaurant and that is this soup – the base of many a noodle dish and dumpling soup. If I buy a duck for duck pancakes, this is the soup I make afterwards.*

Chop the duck carcass, put it into a large pan and cover with 3 litres water. Bring to the boil, then skim off any yuk bits and lower the heat to a simmer. Add all the vegetables, the ginger, star anise and peppercorns and bring back to a simmer for 20 minutes. After the stock has reduced a little and become fragrant, strain it into a clean pot.

Bring the stock back to the boil, then lower the heat to a simmer. Add the fish sauce and sesame oil. Soak and wash the coriander roots and add them to the stock, then infuse over a very low heat for a further 15 minutes. Discard the coriander roots.

Put the noodles into four bowls and pour over the hot stock. Sprinkle over the spring onions, chilli and coriander leaves to serve.

Picking up a bike and cycling is the best way to get around in traffic-clogged Beijing and I took one to visit the city's lakes and wet markets. Hidden in one of the city's old *hutongs* (alleyways) is the famous Li Qun roast duck restaurant. Find it by following the duck!

# NOODLES & RICE

Majestic vehicles that transport the most vibrant of flavours from all over the world, their importance should never be underestimated. Rice and noodles are a staple – eaten every day. It takes a community to grow rice, and without that community there is none. Rice's special status means it is rarely thrown away – eat it for breakfast, throw it into soups, fry or roast.

I learnt to make fresh noodles with Liang Tang at Brickyard, Mutianyu, in the shadow of the Great Wall. The dough is so simple – just flour and water (no eggs), rolled out thin, folded over and cut with a sharp knife into strands.

# NOODLES

The stories of how Marco Polo adopted the dough that the Chinese had long known and used for noodles are well documented, as is the Italians' counterargument that Marco took their pasta to China. It is also said that both nations had their own ways of producing noodles and pasta. Who is right? We will never really know.

Throughout history the noodle, or the dough that makes noodles, has been written about, from as far back as the Jews fleeing Egypt to modern Polish and Russian writings. Many of these doughs were made with potato, flour or ground meal, and were unrefined but bulky and able to take up the sauce or stock with which they were served, making a filling, energy-giving meal.

By contrast, the Far Eastern noodles so much in vogue these days are some of the most refined and easily cooked that you can find. They come in many guises, made with different flours, and with specific uses in mind. Here are some of them (from left to right)…

**Udon noodles** (or sometimes in China, white oil noodles)
These are soft, precooked and ready-to-use noodles perfect for curries,
soups and stir-fries. They are a great storecupboard staple and can
be used for almost anything. The best way to make them hot before
they are dropped into whatever you are making is to pop them in the
microwave for 30 seconds and they will come apart.

**Flat rice noodles** (kway teow or sen yai)
These are used in soups as well as the famous Malaysian Kway Teow
and Thailand's wonderful Phat Thai. Soak in warm water for 20 minutes
before wok frying. These come as seen in the picture and also wider –
use either.

**Glass noodles**
These are usually made of mung beans and are therefore called mung
bean thread or cellophane noodles. They are never fried but are
sometimes used in salads and soups. When hydrating, just cover them
with boiling water and leave for 2 minutes. If adding to soups, they
are first soaked in cold water to reconstitute, then put into a bowl and
covered with soup.

**Dried rice vermicelli**
These are used by Thais in salads, and by the Vietnamese in spring rolls.
They are soaked in warm water for about 30 minutes and are rarely
cooked as they will disintegrate, though they can be deep-fried, when
they become wonderful and crispy.

# PERFECT RICE

ENOUGH FOR 2

*Rice is one of the world's favourite staples, but it is also one of those basics that many people simply cannot perfect. Here is the answer for perfect rice.*

Take a large coffee mug or similar and fill it with rice, then transfer to a pot that has a tight-fitting lid.

Now wash the rice in cold water three times (this stops it from going gluggy/sticky) – do this by placing the pot under cold running water, filling the pot with water and stirring it around, then draining and repeating twice more. Return the washed rice to the pot.

Take the large mug, fill it with cold water and pour over the washed rice, then add a pinch of salt and give it a stir. Shake the pan so the rice is even and add another half mugful of water.

Put the lid on the pot and bring to the boil, then turn the heat down to low and cook for 5 minutes. Now turn the heat off and do not touch it – do not lift the lid or anything. Leave it where it is with the heat off for a further 20 minutes.

Take a fork, lift the lid and run the fork through the cooked rice to ensure it is free-flowing.

Perfect rice, every time.

# MEE GA THI (RICE STICKS WITH COCONUT PORK AND PRAWNS)

**SERVES 2–4**

2 x 400ml tins coconut milk

50ml oil

100g minced pork

100g minced prawns

3 fresh red chillies, roasted and
  de-seeded (see Tip)

2 tablespoons fish sauce

2 tablespoons palm sugar

10g dried shrimps, soaked
  (see Tip on page 154)

150g rice sticks

50g firm tofu

100g beansprouts

50g pickled turnip, drained
  and shredded

a handful of fresh
  coriander leaves

2 fresh red chillies, julienned

Fried Garnish (see page 204)

*Should I feel a little homesick for Asia, these noodles are the antidote.
The top must be piled up with loads of beansprouts, chilli and fried
garnish – loads.*

Heat a wok, add the creamy top layer of the coconut milk and turn up
the heat so it splits. Add the oil and fry the pork and prawns with the
roasted chillies, fish sauce and palm sugar, then add the dried shrimps.

Add half the remaining coconut milk and bring to a simmer, then cook
for 10 minutes until thickened.

In a separate pan, heat the remaining coconut milk and add the rice
sticks. Stir well, then remove from the heat and allow to soften.

Add the tofu to the sauce with the softened rice sticks, heat through
and divide into two or four bowls. Garnish with the beansprouts, pickled
turnip, coriander, chilli and a sprinkle of fried garnish.

Tip
To roast the chillies, roast 2–3 whole dried red chillies in a very hot
220°C/200°C fan/gas 7 oven for 5–10 minutes until they go dark brown
and break up into pieces.

# MALAYSIAN CHAR KWAY TEOW

**ENOUGH FOR 2–4**

300g kway teow (flat rice noodles)

50g pork fat, cut into small cubes, or 50ml vegetable oil

2 banana shallots, sliced

3 garlic cloves, crushed

6 garlic chives, chopped

200g firm tofu, cut into cubes

2 tablespoons kecap manis

2 tablespoons light soy sauce

2 tablespoons dark soy sauce

50g beansprouts

2 eggs, beaten

*This recipe has been put together after many years of eating and sampling and not a lot of cooking. I have always found the best versions on the streets of Penang, but I understand it's not easy to drop in and pick some up, so here goes, this is my version (and there are many versions as this is the equivalent in Malaysia of spaghetti bolognese here). This recipe calls for pork fat as it adds flavour to the noodles, plus cooking oil has always been expensive in large parts of Asia, but you can use vegetable oil if you prefer.*

First soak the noodles in warm water for 20 minutes whilst you make the rest of the dish, then drain.

If using the pork fat, drop the fat into a wok, add 2 tablespoons of water and bring to the boil. Leave the fat to melt over a low heat for 5 minutes, stirring all the time until the pieces of fat are crisp and there is some oil in the wok. If using vegetable oil, heat in a wok until hot.

Turn the heat up, add the shallots and fry quickly, stirring constantly, then add the garlic and cook for a minute, keeping the heat high and the stirring going. Now add the soaked noodles and 50ml water and stir quickly so the shallots and noodles become one. Add the garlic chives and keep cooking and stirring, then add the tofu and half of all the sauces, plus a little more water if the mix is looking a bit dry. Stir well and cook for 2 minutes, keeping the noodles moving.

Drop in the beansprouts and add the eggs, stir well, cook for a further minute, then add the rest of the sauces and remember to keep stirring. Serve immediately.

# SPEEDY FRIED EGG NOODLES

......................................................

**SERVES 4**

splash of vegetable oil

500g fresh yellow egg noodles

a small bunch of spring
   onions, sliced

3 tablespoons oyster sauce

ground white pepper, to taste

dark soy sauce, to taste

3 eggs, beaten

100g beansprouts

*This is a generic noodle with egg recipe and you can use thick or thin
egg noodles – the thinner are usually called Singapore noodles. I like
these noodles because they are fast; my children like them because they
are noodles and are easy to eat. Oh, and they are tasty!*

......................................................

Heat a wok until hot, then add the oil and heat until smoky. Add the
noodles and cook for about 3 minutes until warmed through, moving
them all the time. Add the spring onions and oyster sauce, along with a
little white pepper and some soy sauce, and give it a good stir.

Add the beaten eggs and toss well, then add the beansprouts and
season again with more white pepper and soy sauce. Cook for a minute
or so to soften the beansprouts, stirring, then serve.

# CHIANG MAI NOODLES WITH CHICKEN

**SERVES 4**

500g flat rice noodles

400ml tin coconut milk

1 tablespoon red curry paste
(bought or see page 138)

1 tablespoon palm sugar

4 skinless, boneless chicken
thigh fillets, cut into
small pieces

1 tablespoon fish sauce, or
to taste

200ml vegetable oil

4 small Thai shallots, sliced

1 large fresh red chilli, sliced

a handful of fresh Thai
basil leaves

5 fresh coriander sprigs,
leaves picked

chilli sauce, to serve

*Oh my, I love these. They are a chicken curry noodle one-bowl wonder.
Why they are called Chiang Mai noodles, I am unsure, because in the
north of Thailand very little coconut milk is used as coconuts don't
grow there. Regardless, try it as it's quick, easy and what I think of as
comfort food.*

First soak three-quarters of the noodles in warm water for 20 minutes
whilst you make the rest of the dish, then drain.

In a wok, cook the thick coconut milk from the top layer of the tin over
a medium heat until it splits, then add the red curry paste. Fry for about
5 minutes, until fragrant, then add the palm sugar and continue to cook
for a further 5 minutes until it turns terracotta red in colour and is sticky
like jam.

Add the chicken to the wok, turn to coat in the curry paste, then
cook and colour for a few minutes, stirring all the time. Now add the
remaining coconut milk, bring to the boil and cook for 5 minutes. Stir in
the fish sauce to make it salty.

Meanwhile, heat the vegetable oil in a separate pan until hot, then add
the remaining noodles (these will be used as the garnish) and fry until
crisp. Using a slotted spoon, remove the crisp noodles to kitchen paper
and leave to drain and cool.

In the meantime, in a third pan, plunge the soaked noodles into boiling
water for 1 minute. Divide the boiled noodles among four serving bowls,
then cover each portion with some of the chicken sauce.

Garnish with the shallots, chilli slices, Thai basil and coriander, then
crumble the crisp fried noodles over and serve with a little chilli sauce
on the side.

# KIMCHI FRIED RICE WITH PORK AND EGG

**FEEDS 2 EASILY**

splash of vegetable oil, plus extra for frying the eggs

good knob of butter

6 spring onions, finely chopped

3 rashers smoked bacon, roughly chopped

1 garlic clove, minced

1 tablespoon gochugaru (Korean ground chilli), plus extra to serve

80g kimchi, finely chopped, plus extra to serve

200g cooked white rice, cooled

1 tablespoon good-quality toasted sesame oil

2 tablespoons toasted sesame seeds

2 eggs

*There is rice, there is fried rice and then there is Kimchi Fried Rice. I first made this version for breakfast whilst camping in Korea. It has taken some time to get all the quantities correct, but I think it is now right and ready to publish! The egg on top is a bonus as the yolk makes a sauce that helps to hold it all together. Now if you don't have any leftover cooked rice to hand, you can buy precooked rice; I prefer the Korean version sold in little bowls as it doesn't have any strange taste to it. Older, aged kimchi is so much better than young, fresh kimchi for this recipe.*

Splash a little vegetable oil into a frying pan, set it over a medium heat, then add the butter and leave to melt. Add the spring onions and fry for a minute or so until soft and glossy. Add the bacon and garlic and fry for a minute or two, then sprinkle in the chilli powder. Add the kimchi, keeping the kimchi juice to one side. Fry for 2 minutes – the longer you fry it, the better it will taste.

Add the rice and cook for a good few minutes, stirring all the time, so the rice heats through, adding some kimchi juice if it's a little dry. Turn off the heat, then stir in the sesame oil and seeds.

Fry the eggs in a little oil in a separate small frying pan so that the edges are crisp.

Serve the fried rice and top each portion with a fried egg, sunny side up. The egg is essential here as the runny yolk acts as a sauce and gives a creamy richness to the dish. You can serve with a little extra kimchi on the side and some more ground chilli to sprinkle over. Many Koreans add ketchup and even mayo on top.

# SATAY CHICKEN NOODLES

...............................................

**ENOUGH FOR 3–4 PEOPLE**

50ml vegetable oil

200g chicken, chopped into
  little bits

2 spring onions, finely sliced

500g soft udon noodles

200ml chicken stock or water

a good handful of chopped
  fresh coriander

chilli sauce, to serve

*For the satay sauce*

50ml vegetable oil

1 small Thai shallot, diced

1 tablespoon red curry paste
  (bought or see page 138)

2 small fresh red chillies, de-
  seeded and finely chopped

300g ground peanuts or
  crunchy peanut butter

50ml soy sauce

*I am, and always will be, a sucker for noodles. This is not a side dish, this is a big bowl of feed-your-face food. I like to make enough for three to four people and always have some left over as it is just as delicious cold. You can also use minced pork or even tofu for this one. Try making your own satay sauce or buy a jar (try Jimmy's).*

...............................................

To make the satay sauce, put a medium saucepan over heat and add the oil. Leave to warm and then add the shallot, frying gently for 3 minutes. Add the curry paste and then the chopped chilli. Stirring constantly, cook the paste for 5 minutes until fragrant. Add the peanuts and 200ml water and stir well, then bring to the boil. Add the soy and stir. Remove from the heat and leave to cool. You can store this for weeks in a sterilised jar in the fridge.

Heat the wok and get it really hot, then add the oil and, when it shimmers, add the chicken and cook for a minute, then turn it and cook again for another minute.

Add the spring onions and mix them all in together with the chicken. The chicken will now be cooked, so act quickly so it doesn't dry out.

Add the noodles and stir them into the chicken. As they start to get hot, run half the stock or water down the side of the wok and let the stock boil, stirring it really well and keeping the heat high. The noodles will start to separate and plump up and bloat, which is a sign of them getting hot and taking up the moisture.

Add 100g of the satay sauce and a little more stock and stir it well. If it is really sticking, add more water.

Serve in big bowls with the coriander sprinkled over, spoons, chopsticks and a bib and chilli sauce on the side.

# SAMGYETANG (KOREAN CHICKEN FILLED WITH RICE)

**SERVES 4**

70g short grain sweet glutinous rice

50g ginseng root

10 jujubes (optional)

10 garlic cloves, chopped

1 medium oven-ready chicken or 4 small chickens (poussins)

3 spring onions

salt and ground white pepper

*This is one of those yin and yang recipes and is traditionally eaten on the three hottest days of the year, known in Korea as SAM. It is served in specialist restaurants, usually as a single portion, but I have given the option here of making one big pot instead. Samgyetang is usually not seasoned and is served with salt and white pepper alongside instead – this way it can be seasoned to your own taste and you can dip bits of chicken into the salt and pepper for flavour.*

Wash the rice in cold water to remove any excess starch, then drain and put it into a bowl with enough cold water to cover. Leave to soak for 30 minutes, then drain and set to one side.

Roughly chop half the ginseng and put it into a bowl to make the stuffing. Put the rest aside for the stock pot.

Chop half the jujubes for the stuffing and put the other half aside for the stock pot.

Add half the garlic to the bowl for the stuffing and put the rest with the stock pot ingredients.

Drain the rice and mix with all the reserved stuffing ingredients, then put to one side.

Now prep the chicken(s). Remove the excess fat (parson's nose) to make sure the broth is nice and clear. Tuck the neck skin underneath the chicken to ensure the stuffing doesn't fall out (or alternatively, skewer the end). Stuff the chicken with the stuffing mix, then cross its legs by threading each leg through incisions in the skin on the opposite side. This helps to seal the rice mix inside the chicken. Put into a stock pot.

Add the remaining jujubes, ginseng and garlic to the pan with enough water (about 3 litres) to cover the chicken. Bring to the boil, then place a lid on the pan. Reduce the heat and simmer for 1½ hours, or until the chicken is cooked.

Roughly chop the spring onions and add the white parts to the pot. Simmer for an additional 3–4 minutes until they are wilted. Meanwhile, finely chop the green parts of the spring onions.

Sprinkle the finely chopped spring onions over the top just before serving. Serve in one large hot bowl, or individual hot bowls for the smaller chickens, with small dishes of salt and white pepper alongside for seasoning.

# BIBIMBAP

· · · · · · · · · · · · · · · · · · · · · · · · · · ·

## SERVES 2

300g cooked short grain or
basmati rice

*For the beansprouts*
100g soya bean sprouts
  or beansprouts
1 teaspoon good-quality
  sesame oil
1 teaspoon toasted
  sesame seeds
pinch of salt

*For the spinach*
60g young spinach leaves
1 teaspoon good-quality
  sesame oil
1 teaspoon toasted
  sesame seeds
pinch of salt

*For the carrot*
1 teaspoon vegetable oil
1 carrot, peeled and cut
  into julienne
pinch of salt

*For the courgette*
1 teaspoon vegetable oil
1 courgette, halved lengthways
  and thinly sliced
pinch of salt

*For the mushrooms*
1 teaspoon vegetable oil
60g straw mushrooms or
  enoki mushrooms
pinch of salt

and (opposite page)…

*This is the most famous dish in Korea! It is usually served in a special bowl, which is heated first (as the rice and all the garnishes are cold), then everything is mixed in the bowl and that is how it's heated. I have eaten Bibimbap in many places, but the best was in a restaurant in Jonju where it was served in a heavy gold bowl; it was amazing. This recipe is a guide. It's always very pretty before it's mixed, the ingredients organised in a Catherine wheel formation or a clock face. In Korea it's a dish using leftovers, which has now been glamorised. It should contain rice, some vegetables and an egg or egg yolk, cooked or not, for good measure. There must also be the ever-important gochujang, or Korean chilli paste, served alongside. Unlike in many other Asian countries, in Korea vegetables and sprouts are always cooked, pickled or made into kimchi (brined and cured), so that's why all the toppings need to be cooked. It's said to be better for the digestion.*

· · · · · · · · · · · · · · · · · · · · · · · · · · · · · · · · · · · · · · · · · · · · · · · · · ·

If you don't have Korean stone bowls, keep the rice hot while you prepare the rest of the dish.

Remove any skins from the heads of the bean sprouts and cut off any roots. Put them into a bowl, cover with boiling water and leave for 5 minutes until softened. Cool the bean sprouts under cold running water, then drain and shake away any water. Mix with the sesame oil, sesame seeds and salt, then set to one side.

Pinch off the leaves of the spinach. Discard the stems, then put the leaves into a bowl and cover with boiling water. Leave to wilt for 30 seconds, then drain and squeeze out any excess water. Lightly season with the sesame oil, sesame seeds and salt, then set to one side.

For the carrot, heat the vegetable oil in a small frying pan over a high heat, then add the carrot and fry for 1½ minutes until just softened. Season with the salt, then set to one side. Repeat with the courgette and then the mushrooms, setting both to one side once cooked.

And then…

# BIBIMBAP
(continued)

**For the beef**
100g bulgogi beef, thinly sliced
(or thinly sliced sirloin steak)
2 teaspoons soy sauce
1 teaspoon good-quality
sesame oil
1 teaspoon toasted
sesame seeds
pinch of sugar
1 tablespoon vegetable oil

**For the chilli sauce**
3 tablespoons gochujang
(Korean chilli paste)
1 tablespoon soy sauce
1 teaspoon minced garlic
2 tablespoons good-quality
sesame oil
2 spring onions, finely chopped

**To finish and serve**
2 eggs or 2 egg yolks
a little vegetable oil, for
frying (optional)
2 teaspoons good-quality
sesame oil (to brush the
inside of the bowl)

In a bowl, mix the beef with the soy sauce, sesame oil, sesame seeds and sugar. Heat the vegetable oil in a frying pan over a medium heat, then add the beef, cooking and stirring it for a minute or so until it's just done. Remove from the heat and set to one side.

If using Korean stone bowls, heat over a high heat until they are hot. Meanwhile, mix all the chilli sauce ingredients together in a small bowl.

To finish, fry the eggs to your liking in a frying pan with a little vegetable oil and set to one side, or you can serve raw egg yolks if you prefer.

To serve, pour the sesame oil into the hot stone bowls and use a pastry brush to coat the insides. Place the rice in the centre of each bowl and assemble the vegetables and beef in neat sections. Add a dollop of the chilli sauce, then the fried eggs or raw yolks on top. Serve sizzling hot, with the remaining chilli sauce on the side.

*Picture on pages 196–197*

# PUMPKIN NOODLES WITH LIME PICKLE

**SERVES 6**

80ml vegetable oil

100g red curry paste (bought or see page 138)

30g palm sugar

2 medium butternut squash, peeled, de-seeded and cut into 4–5cm chunks

2 x 400ml tins coconut milk

175ml creamed coconut

1 tablespoon fish sauce

2 tablespoons lime pickle

3 lemongrass stalks, bruised

500g pre-cooked egg noodles

100g beansprouts

Fried Garnish (see page 204)

a small bunch of fresh coriander, leaves picked

*A long time ago a group of friends were coming round for dinner and I was going to cook a Thai curry. I had, however, forgotten to buy any meat to go into the curry, and that is how this noodle dish was born. I still love it and make it whenever I can. I have even put it on the menu on occasion. In Thailand this would be made with pumpkin and if you can find a good one, use that. If not, butternut squash works well. The addition of lime pickle was a last-minute thing because I wanted a little more sour and hot as the pumpkin is sweet. As a result the finished dish was fragrant, sweet, sour, hot and salty, with all the flavours taken up by the floury rich noodles.*

Pour the oil into a wok and add the red curry paste. Fry for 2 minutes, then add the palm sugar and let it cook with the curry paste for 4 minutes until sticky and fragrant. Add the squash, stir well and cook for 2–3 minutes, then pour in the coconut milk and creamed coconut, season with the fish sauce and add the lime pickle and lemongrass.

Bring to the boil and cook over a medium heat for about 20–30 minutes until the squash is soft but not mushy, stirring occasionally.

Put the noodles into a heatproof bowl and pour boiling water over them to reheat. Leave for 2 minutes, then drain.

Divide the noodles among the serving bowls, then spoon a few squash pieces over the top of each portion. Top with the beansprouts and pour some of the remaining squash with its sauce over the top.

Garnish with the fried garnish and the coriander.

# LA LA CHILLI AND FAT NOODLES

**ENOUGH FOR 2**

*For the sambal oelek*

5 dried red chillies

1 large onion, chopped

10 fresh red chillies, half left
 whole and half de-seeded

5 fresh green chillies,
 de-seeded

juice of 4 limes

40g belachan (shrimp paste),
 toasted (see Tip on
 page 138)

*For the la la*

4 tablespoons vegetable oil

250g fresh small clams, cleaned

200g ho fun (wide Chinese
 rice noodles)

75g beansprouts

75g crispy fried onions

*On the streets of Chinatown in Kuala Lumpur I discovered la la or 'little clams'. And wow, are they good. You can use any small clams you like – just clean them by soaking in cold water for a few hours before you cook. How could clams be so beautiful? You can either make the sambal or buy it.*

To make the sambal, first soak the dried chillies in hot water for 20 minutes to soften, then drain. Put all the ingredients into a food processor and blend together until smooth.

Heat a large wok with a lid and add the vegetable oil. Once it's hot, add 2 tablespoons of the sambal paste and cook for 2–3 minutes, then add the clams and 50ml water and cook for a further 4–6 minutes.

Quickly blast the ho fun noodles in the microwave to help loosen and separate them, then drop into the wok and cook for a couple of minutes. Add the beansprouts and give it all a good toss. Discard any clams that remain closed.

Spoon the la la into two bowls and top with the crispy onions to serve.

# NAENGMYEON (CHILLED KOREAN NOODLES)

**FOR 2 PEOPLE**

*For the beef stock*

500g beef brisket

150g Korean radish (moo) or daikon radish, scrubbed and cut into big chunks

3 large spring onions, roughly chopped

1 onion, quartered

30g fresh root ginger, peeled and snapped into chunks

5 garlic cloves, peeled

pinch of salt

*For the noodles and broth*

250g dried naengmyeon noodles or buckwheat noodles

3 tablespoons soy sauce

2 tablespoons apple cider vinegar

1 teaspoon sugar

10 ice cubes

*To garnish*

1 egg

½ cucumber, half peeled and cut into julienne

½ nashi (Asian) pear, peeled, cored and sliced into long thin slivers

1 fresh red chilli, finely sliced

mustard and apple cider vinegar, to serve

*Eaten all over Korea, these noodles are made in homes and restaurants and are served with lots of ice – yes, cold noodles. They are, however, eaten in winter, not in summer as you might imagine, because it is believed that if you have hot in hot weather and cold in cold weather it can help to regulate your body temperature – yin and yang.*

Put all the stock ingredients, except the salt, into a large saucepan with 1.25 litres water. Cover and bring to the boil, then reduce the heat and simmer for about 1 hour, occasionally skimming the impurities off the top as it cooks.

While the beef cooks, add the noodles to a pot of boiling water and cook as per the packet instructions. When the noodles start to float to the surface, they're done. Once cooked, rinse them under cold water and drain.

Once the stock is ready, remove the beef. Wrap it tightly in clingfilm to keep it moist and put it to one side to cool. Strain the stock, pour into a container and chill in the fridge for 1 hour.

Make a thin omelette in a frying pan using one egg. Remove it from the pan, then roll it up and slice into thin strips. Prep the cucumber, pear and chilli.

Slice the beef into wafer-thin strips and sprinkle the pinch of salt on top.

Remove the stock from the fridge and skim off any fat so that the broth is clear. Stir in the soy sauce, vinegar and sugar.

Pile the cooked noodles into a bowl, then add the beef and ladle the broth over. Top the noodles and beef with the omelette, cucumber, pear and chilli garnishes. Finally, add the ice cubes to the broth.

Serve with mustard and apple cider vinegar on the side.

# MALAY NOODLES
# WITH SUGAR SNAPS AND KECAP MANIS

.........................................................................................

**SERVES LOTS**

*For the paste*

100g peeled fresh root ginger

100g peeled garlic cloves

100g fresh coriander root,
washed and soaked


*For the noodle mix*

100ml vegetable oil

1kg pre-cooked white thick
noodles or udon noodles

200g sugar snap peas

100g beansprouts

100ml soy sauce

100ml kecap manis

50ml fish sauce


*To garnish*

bunch of fresh coriander,
leaves picked

Fried Garnish (see page 204)
or crispy fried onions

*This was taught to me by a chef friend's Malaysian wife and these noodles became a staple of mine for years. They are the quickest of the quick. You must search out the sweet kecap manis.*

.........................................................................................

To make the paste, pound all the ingredients to a paste and leave to one side.

Heat the vegetable oil in a wok until shimmering, then add the ginger/garlic paste and stir until fragrant. Add the noodles and stir-fry for about 2 minutes, then add the sugar snaps and beansprouts. Toss well and cook for a further minute. Add the soy sauce, kecap manis and fish sauce and toss together well.

To serve, combine the coriander and fried garnish, then sprinkle over the top of the noodles and serve.

# FRIED GARNISH

. . . . . . . . . . . . . . . . . . . . . . . . . . . . . .

**MAKES ENOUGH TO
GARNISH A FEW DISHES**

200ml vegetable oil

6 long fresh red chillies, sliced
   on the diagonal

10 small Thai shallots,
   thinly sliced

1 bulb of garlic, cloves peeled
   and thinly sliced

*It may sound like a bit of work, but these little gems are something to
behold. I first came across them on the streets of Bangkok. I sat and
watched a lady making kilos of each before she opened her stall to the
hungry hordes. The trick is in the temperature of the oil. If you start from
cold, then the water contained in the vegetables evaporates before the
sugars start to caramelise, resulting in crisp but not burnt shallots, garlic
and chillies, all of which can be stored in airtight tins or tubs lined with a
little greaseproof paper for later use (the paper will absorb any moisture).*

Pour the vegetable oil into a wok, add the chillies to the cold oil, then
turn the heat on. The chillies will soon start to bubble, but make sure
you keep the heat at a level so that it bubbles steadily but not frantically
(the temperature of the oil must stay below 160°C). You want the chillies
to fry and the water to evaporate, but you don't want the sugars to
caramelise, so the chillies will become crisp-fried but remain bright red
(if the oil gets too hot, the chillies will burn and be bitter) – this will take
a good 10 minutes or so, turning occasionally.

Using a slotted spoon, transfer the fried chillies to a plate lined with
kitchen paper and leave to cool.

Let the oil cool again a little and repeat the same process separately with
the shallots and garlic slices.

Once cool, store the garnishes in airtight tubs in a cool place for up to
3 weeks and use as required.

# NASI LAMAK (MALAYSIAN RICE AND SAMBAL)

**ENOUGH TO FEED A FAMILY**

*For the nasi lamak*
500g jasmine rice or
  basmati rice
250ml coconut water (from
  the inside of the coconut,
  not milk)
2 small Thai shallots, sliced
2cm piece of fresh root ginger,
  peeled and bruised
2 lemongrass stalks, bruised
1 screw pine leaf or a stem
  of curry leaves
caster sugar and salt, to taste

*For the prawn sambal*
2–3 tablespoons vegetable oil
6 tablespoons dried chilli paste
10 small Thai shallots
4 garlic cloves
4 candlenuts or
  macadamia nuts (optional)
1 teaspoon belachan (shrimp
  paste), toasted (see Tip on
  page 138)
2 lemongrass stalks, bruised
1 tablespoon concentrated
  cooking tamarind
500g fresh raw prawns,
  peeled, deveined and
  halved lengthways
2–4 tablespoons sugar
salt
sliced spring onions, to garnish
  (optional)

*To serve*
5 hard-boiled eggs, peeled
  and halved
ikan bilis (deep-fried crispy
  anchovies)
½ cucumber, sliced
deep-fried peanuts, skins on
  (optional)

*This is the most classic of all the classic Malaysian rice dishes. It is all about the sambal. Each family, area, town and region has its own. Some are very powerful with dried shrimps, others are fabulously hot – this one sits somewhere in between, so do what you will and enjoy playing around. Make it as spicy as you like.*

To cook the nasi lamak, put all the ingredients into a saucepan along with 425ml water, put a lid on, bring to the boil and simmer for 5 minutes. Turn off the heat and let sit for 20 minutes (don't lift the lid).

While the rice is cooking, make the prawn sambal. Heat the vegetable oil in a wok until hot, then add the dried chilli paste and fry over a medium heat until fragrant or until you can see the oil separate/split from the paste (it's important to maintain a steady heat).

Blend together the shallots, garlic and candlenuts in a food processor, then add to the wok with the shrimp paste and 125ml water. Add the lemongrass and tamarind. Stir the sambal until it thickens, then add the prawns, sugar and some salt. Leave it for a few minutes, then remove from the heat. You can garnish your sambal with sliced spring onions, if you like.

Serve the nasi lamak with the hard-boiled eggs, deep-fried crispy anchovies, sliced cucumber and peanuts, with the prawn sambal (sambal udang).

# PHAT THAI

· · · · · · · · · · · · · · · · · · · · · · · · · ·

**FEEDS 6**

600g thick flat rice noodles

a bunch of fresh coriander
with roots

20 garlic cloves, finely chopped

100ml vegetable oil

20 medium fresh raw
prawns, peeled

150g pickled turnip, drained
and chopped

30g sugar

50ml concentrated
cooking tamarind

4 eggs, beaten

2 tablespoons oyster sauce

50ml fish sauce

100g beansprouts

1 lime, juiced

1 bunch of spring onions, cut
at an angle

100g roasted peanuts, crushed

3 fresh red chillies, de-seeded
and sliced

crispy fried onions, to serve

*You must, must try this!*

*Phat Thai, pronounced Pad Thai, is central Thailand's greatest snack food. Sold in hawkers' markets within Bangkok and in the many towns that surround it, it is never very spicy; the chillies are added at the end, usually by the consumer, sometimes along with other ingredients set out on tables. To me the special ingredient is pickled turnip, which you can buy from Asian stores, and which gives the noodles that extra sour dimension and crunchy texture. Add the lime at the last minute, and replace the prawns with thin strips of chicken breast if you want (fry it for an extra 4 minutes or so, until cooked through). Or you can even make the dish without either prawns or chicken. Any which way, I could eat Phat Thai every day, as indeed I did when travelling around Thailand.*

· · · · · · · · · · · · · · · · · · · · · · · · · · · · · · · · · · · · · · · · · · · · · ·

Soak the rice noodles in warm water for 20 minutes, then drain and keep to one side.

Pick the leaves from the coriander and reserve. Soak and wash the coriander roots, then pound the roots and garlic together using a mortar and pestle (use the coriander stems if you have no roots, otherwise discard them).

Heat the vegetable oil in a wok or deep frying pan over a high heat and when it's shimmering, add the pounded garlic and coriander roots. Stir for a few moments, then add the prawns and half the pickled turnip. Cook for 30 seconds, then add the sugar and tamarind. Add the noodles and toss, then add the eggs and stir-fry for a further 2 minutes.

Pour in the oyster sauce and fish sauce and toss to mix, then stir-fry for 4–5 minutes. Add half the beansprouts and finally finish off with the lime juice, half the spring onions and half the peanuts.

Pile the noodles into a large serving dish and garnish with the remaining turnip, beansprouts, spring onion and roasted peanuts and the coriander leaves, chillies and crispy fried onions.

# BBQ & GRILLS

I learnt to barbecue as a kid in Melbourne, but realised much later on in Argentina how to do it properly. The Koreans have their own methods, as do the Japanese, and there are the street grills for satay in Penang and Bangkok. This is what I know. Beware the flame because it burns. Be kind to the glowing embers and they will be kind to you.

# VIETNAMESE GRILLED BEEF
# WITH GLASS NOODLE SALAD

......................................................

**SERVES 4**

300g glass noodles
(mung bean thread or
cellophane noodles)

2 tablespoons vegetable oil

2 small Thai shallots,
finely sliced

1 garlic clove, finely sliced

1 cucumber, shredded

crispy fried onions, to sprinkle

2 x 175g sirloin steaks

15g fresh mint

15g fresh Thai basil

15g fresh coriander

salt and freshly ground
black pepper

*For the dressing*

juice of 3 limes

1 garlic clove, finely chopped

2 small Thai shallots,
finely chopped

2 fresh long red chillies,
finely chopped

40g palm sugar

40ml fish sauce

30g fresh coriander root,
soaked and washed

*As a cook I travel and pick up ideas, mixing and matching things that
I have discovered in different places to make a single dish. This recipe
is not in any way traditional, but it is really tasty and light and not that
difficult. I like the beef to be a little charred, for added flavour.*

......................................................

Soak the glass noodles in boiling water for 2 minutes until hydrated,
then drain.

Make the dressing by pounding the lime juice, garlic, Thai shallots,
red chilli, palm sugar, fish sauce and the coriander roots together to a
dressing consistency.

Heat half the oil in a wok and fry the shallots and garlic for 1 minute until
golden. Drain well.

Combine the shredded cucumber with the drained noodles and mix in
the dressing. Sprinkle the crispy fried onions over the top.

Using a pair of scissors, snip the fat of the steaks eight or ten times (this
is so the steaks don't shrivel and go dry). Oil the steaks very well with
the remaining oil and season with a little salt and pepper. Heat a griddle
pan or have a BBQ ready and glowing hot.

Cook the steaks on one side for 3 minutes, making sure they are always
on a high heat, then turn the steaks and repeat. Remove from the heat
and leave to rest for 5 minutes. Slice as thinly as possible, toss with the
salad and serve with the fresh herbs.

# LANGOUSTINES IN CHILLI JAM

**ENOUGH FOR 4 OR MAYBE 2**

*For the chilli jam*

750g red onions, chopped

2 large red peppers, diced

1 bulb of garlic, cloves peeled
and sliced

200g long fresh red chillies,
de-seeded

vegetable oil, for frying

250g cherry tomatoes, halved

100g dried shrimps, soaked
(see Tip on page 154)

100ml fish sauce

200g palm sugar

12 langoustines, split

4 teaspoons vegetable oil

50ml crème fraîche

*I am a sucker for chilli jam. It is not like the jam you spread on toast, more of a chutney consistency. The reason I have used langoustines is because I love them, but you can use prawns – big ones if possible. You don't have to make the jam as there are a few different ones available in speciality shops, however, the quantity the recipe makes is large and the jam will store in jars for a good couple of months.*

To make the chilli jam, fry the onion, pepper, garlic and chillies in oil over a medium heat until soft but without colour, stirring all the time – it should take a good 10 minutes. Add the tomatoes and cook until softened, then turn up the heat and give it all a bit of colour.

In a food processor, blend the cooked ingredients and add the dried shrimps, fish sauce and palm sugar until a rough paste forms.

Put the mix back into the pot, return to the stove and cook for 40 minutes over a low heat until the mixture becomes a dark red and sticky jam. This makes two jars of jam, which will store for a couple of months in the fridge.

Heat a griddle pan until very hot or have the coals on the BBQ glowing.

Brush the open side of the langoustines with the oil and grill flesh-side down for 3 minutes. Turn when they come away from the pan and let cook for 3 more minutes, until the shells start to smell like they are roasting (you will know).

In a wok heat 100g of the chilli jam, drop the cooked langoustines into the wok and toss well.

Serve with a little crème fraîche on the side.

# MACKEREL, SPINACH, SESAME AND MISO

SERVES 6

6 nice-sized mackerel fillets, skin on

dashi or miso soup (mixed according to packet instructions), for wilting the spinach, plus 3 tablespoons for the dressing

500g spinach

50g sesame seeds, plus extra to coat the spinach

2 teaspoons sugar

2 tablespoons dark soy sauce

1 lemon, sliced, to serve

*For the marinade*

2 tablespoons lemon juice

4 tablespoons light soy sauce

4 tablespoons sake

*Oily fish like mackerel and tuna work wonders over flame because the oil keeps the fish moist and a little scorched to give a nice char and a touch of bitterness. That bitterness is fantastic with this as the sesame seeds are sweet and smoky. The whole thing is then finished off with a light Japanese glaze.*

Put the fillets into a non-reactive bowl, then mix together the marinade ingredients and pour over. Leave for about 2 hours, turning the fish halfway through.

Bring a pan of dashi or miso soup to the boil, drop in the spinach and cook for about 1 minute, just enough to wilt it, then drain.

Toast the sesame seeds in a dry pan until golden. Using a mortar and pestle, crush the seeds with the sugar. Mix well with the soy sauce and extra dashi or miso soup until you have a smooth dressing. Add the spinach and work lightly into a solid mass.

Divide the spinach into six pieces and roll each one into a little cylinder. Dip one end into the toasted sesame seeds to coat, then arrange on your serving plate.

Preheat a griddle pan or BBQ to hot and cook the mackerel, skin side up first, for about 3 minutes each side until it blisters and the fish is cooked, basting occasionally with the marinade. Serve with the spinach and garnish with slices of lemon.

# ROTI BREAD WITH GRILLED LAMB

. . . . . . . . . . . . . . . . . . . . . . . . . . . . . . . . . . .

**ENOUGH FOR ABOUT
8 PORTIONS**

*For the lamb*

4 lamb rumps or a leg of lamb
   cut into 8 pieces at the seam
   (your butcher can do this)

1 tablespoon salt

juice of 3 lemons

*For the paste*

½ tablespoon cardamom pods

½ tablespoon whole cloves

½ tablespoon ground turmeric

250g live full-fat yoghurt

2 fresh red chillies, chopped

3 stems of fresh curry leaves

4 garlic cloves, grated

1 tablespoon ground cinnamon

1 teaspoon salt

1 teaspoon freshly ground
   black pepper

*Smoking grills piled with hunks of meat as the sun goes down at the
Ramadan markets in Malaysia were always a welcome sight. In particular
the lamb, usually served with flat breads and pickled onions, is simple
and delicious. This is pretty easy to replicate at home; however, you will
have to settle for cooler nights as those days were always above 35°C
with 85 per cent humidity.*

. . . . . . . . . . . . . . . . . . . . . . . . . . . . . . . . . . . . . . . . . . . . . .

You first need to tenderise the lamb. Score the fat deeply and then rub
the lamb all over with the salt and the lemon juice. Leave to sit for an
hour or so.

Toast the cardamom, cloves and turmeric in a dry frying pan to release
their aroma, then grind to a powder in a mortar and pestle.

Put the yoghurt and chillies, curry leaves and all the toasted spices in
a food processor with the garlic, cinnamon, salt and pepper to make a
paste (alternatively, you could just flavour the yoghurt with some ground
cumin or garam masala, again first toasted briefly in a dry pan).

Rub the yoghurt mix all over the salted lamb, mixing the yoghurt and
lemon juice together. Leave the lamb in the fridge overnight, giving it a
turn every so often.

The next day, get the griddle pan or BBQ ready and make the rotis
(see opposite).

Barbecue the lamb for about 30 minutes, brushing with more of the
yoghurt mix along the way so that it gets a nice crust. Leave it to rest for
about 10 minutes before slicing it.

# ROTIS

..........................................

**MAKES ABOUT 12 GOOD-SIZED BREADS**

1 teaspoon salt

1 teaspoon sugar

150ml milk

1 teaspoon fresh yeast

60g ghee or clarified butter

150g natural yoghurt

500g plain flour

50ml melted ghee or clarified butter, to finish

Put the salt, sugar, 30ml of the milk and the yeast into a large bowl and mix well. Leave and let the yeast dissolve and start to work.

Heat the remaining milk with the ghee or clarified butter until it reaches blood temperature, then take off the heat and add the yoghurt.

Mix the yoghurt with the yeast and stir well. Add the flour and knead for 5 minutes into a dough – it should be soft and elastic. Leave to prove for 30 minutes or until doubled in size. Divide the dough into 12 even-sized balls, cover and leave for 15 minutes.

Once the griddle pan or BBQ is hot, roll each piece of dough into a long sausage shape, rub the whole thing with some of the melted ghee and roll up into a snail shape. Flatten the rolled-up dough by patting the dough between your hands with a little flour so it's very thin.

Put a roti in the pan or BBQ and let it cook for 2 minutes, turning when it is coloured. Take from the heat when it smells cooked and brush with some more ghee, squashing and crumpling the roti up in your hands. Really, it's that easy. Cook the rest of the rotis.

# WHOLE SPATCHCOCKED CHICKEN
# WITH LEMON AND HERBS

**FEEDS 4**

4 little chooks

10 garlic cloves, crushed

1 teaspoon flaked salt

200ml olive oil

juice of 2 lemons

a handful of picked fresh
   rosemary leaves, chopped

a large handful of fresh
   flat-leaf parsley

a large handful of oregano
   or marjoram

*This is such a Australian BBQ recipe. I grew up in Melbourne, where whole communities of Greeks and Italians had settled in the 1950s. These influences resulted in amazing food, much of it cooked over flame. This recipe can be used for a big chicken or these little ones, which I like very much. Spatchcocking a chicken is really easy – see my method below or ask your butcher.*

To spatchcock the chickens, take a pair of strong scissors or poultry shears, cut down either side of the backbone of each chicken and take the backbone out. Turn upside down and flatten, cracking the bones but leaving them in.

Take the spatchcocked chickens and, using a sharp knife, score and stab the skin to allow the marinade to penetrate. Lay the boned thighs out flat in a large dish ready to marinate. Mix the garlic with the salt, 100ml of the olive oil and all the lemon juice and chopped rosemary. Rub the chickens well with the mix and leave for an hour or so.

Preheat the BBQ or a griddle pan.

In a food processor, blend the parsley and oregano or marjoram with the remaining olive oil. Pour half this mix over the chickens when ready to cook and give it a good stir around.

Put the marinated chickens over the hot coals or griddle pan, in batches, and give them a good blast of heat, then turn after 2 minutes. Lift them a little higher away from the heat if using a BBQ and cook for 15 minutes or so more, turning often, until cooked through.

Take from the heat and place in a large flat serving dish. Serve with the remaining herb oil poured over or alongside.

# COD WITH MISO AND GREEN BEAN SALAD

**FEEDS 4**

4 cod fillets, about 250g each

200g green beans

2 long spring onions,
    thinly sliced

2 teaspoons black
    sesame seeds

*For the marinade*

50ml sake

75ml mirin

225g white miso paste

110g granulated sugar

*Cod with miso has been made famous by Nobu. It's his signature and a delicious dish it is – I have eaten variations all over the world, from Sydney to Clapham and from New York to the Maldives. I like mine done over coals, which I reckon adds a bit of Aussie to it.*

First make the marinade. Bring the sake and mirin to the boil in a medium saucepan over a high heat. Boil for 20 seconds to evaporate the alcohol.

Turn the heat down to low and add the miso paste, mixing with a wooden spoon. When the miso has dissolved completely, turn the heat up to high again and add the sugar, stirring constantly with the wooden spoon to ensure the bottom of the pan doesn't burn. Remove from the heat once the sugar is fully dissolved. Cool to room temperature.

Pat the cod fillets thoroughly dry with paper towels. Slather the fish with the marinade, reserving some to serve on the side, place in a non-reactive dish or bowl and cover tightly with clingfilm. Leave to steep in the fridge overnight or longer.

Bring a large pot of water to the boil, drop in the beans and cook for 2 minutes until soft. Drain and whilst still hot, drop in the spring onions and stir well so they wilt. Add 1 tablespoon of the miso mix and stir, then sprinkle with the black sesame seeds.

Heat the BBQ or a griddle pan. Lightly wipe off any excess miso clinging to the fillets, but don't rinse it off. Put the fish on the BBQ skin-side up. Cover with a bowl or similar and cook for 6 minutes, then take away the bowl and cook for 2 more minutes until lightly charred. Peel the skin off, then serve the fish the other way round on top of the bean salad, with the reserved miso on the side.

Tip
This marinade also works wonders with lamb cutlets and steaks.

Back to Australia and ordering a take-away from B.B.Q. King in Sydney – home to the best Chinese duck! Cooking goat curry over an open fire cowboy-style in a Queensland cattle station and going out to the Great Barrier Reef.

# PRAWNS WITH LIME AND TAMARIND

...........................................................

**FEEDS 4**

12 medium fresh prawns, shell on

1 banana leaf, to serve

*For the salad*

4 small Thai shallots, finely sliced lengthways

2 shallots or white onions, finely sliced lengthways

2 lemongrass stalks, outer leaves removed and inner leaves very finely sliced

5 lime leaves, finely sliced

1 knuckle of fresh root ginger, cut into julienne

2 fresh red chillies, de-seeded and cut into julienne

a handful of fresh coriander leaves

a small handful of fresh mint leaves

*For the dressing*

60g palm sugar

2 tablespoons fresh lime juice

2 tablespoons fish sauce

1 tablespoon concentrated cooking tamarind

*As prawns cook, all I can think of is sunshine and sand. The smell of grilled or barbecued prawns either means the summer has come or that I am standing in a market in the south of Thailand and it is properly hot.*

*These are simple enough to cook – just buy good-quality prawns, even if it is just one per person, because great prawns taste of prawns, but cheap ones taste of very little. The shell must be on to protect the delicate flesh, but also the flavour from the shells is what makes a prawn taste like a prawn. You get in a bit of a mess, but it is going to be worth it, I promise.*

...........................................................

With a sharp knife or a pair of scissors, cut through the shell between the legs of each prawn to make them easier to peel.

Preheat a griddle pan or BBQ until hot, then cook the prawns for about 3 minutes on each side until nicely pink and the shells are just catching.

Meanwhile, for the salad, just mix all the salad ingredients together in a bowl and scrunch them in your hands to release all the fragrances and oils.

For the dressing, put the palm sugar, lime juice and fish sauce into a bowl and stir to dissolve the sugar, then stir in the tamarind. Add some of the dressing to the salad, then drop in the hot grilled prawns and mix together.

Serve on the banana leaf, with a small bowlful of the remaining dressing on the side.

*Pictures also on pages 230–231*

# WHOLE BREAM, POMELO AND HERB SALAD

............................................................................

**SERVES 4–6**

1.2kg whole sea bream, split and butterflied (get your fishmonger to split the fish in half like a kipper cut)

vegetable oil, for brushing

*For the salad*

1 large pomelo

2 spring onions, cut diagonally

1 or 2 fresh red chillies, cut into fine julienne

20g pickled ginger, cut into julienne

½ cucumber, cut into julienne

a small bunch of fresh mint, leaves picked

a small bunch of fresh coriander, leaves picked

2 small Thai shallots, finely diced

zest of ½ lime

*For the dressing*

2 teaspoons fresh lime juice

2 teaspoons coconut vinegar

1½ teaspoons fish sauce

1 teaspoon sugar

1 teaspoon good-quality sesame oil

1 teaspoon peanut oil

4 teaspoons toasted sesame seeds

*Cooking a whole fish over flame can be tricky, but having watched the Chinese split their fish and butterfly it, I now cook mine their way. The salad is a herb salad and the pomelo is the citrus that keeps the fish on its toes. I also like this served with a little nam prik dipping sauce (see page 81), made with fish sauce and fresh chillies.*

............................................................................

Prepare the pomelo by peeling it and then segmenting. Discard the peel and the bits that are not just fruit. Mix all the rest of the salad ingredients with the pomelo.

Mix all the dressing ingredients together.

Brush the fish with vegetable oil and cook over a high heat on a BBQ or griddle pan for 5 minutes, flesh-side down, then turn over and cook for another 5 minutes.

Lift the whole fish onto a large plate, then dress the salad and pour it over the fish.

Done.

# MALACCA PORK SATAY
# WITH PINEAPPLE AND PEANUT SAUCE

**MAKES 20 SKEWERS**

*For the pork skewers*

½ teaspoon each ground coriander, ground cumin and ground turmeric

3 small Thai shallots, chopped

2 lemongrass stalks, outer leaves removed and inner stalks chopped

4 garlic cloves, chopped

1 thumb-sized piece of fresh root ginger, peeled and chopped

20g palm sugar

good pinch of salt

1 tablespoon vegetable oil

800g pork tenderloin, cut into thin ribbons

*For the satay sauce*

6 dried red chillies, de-seeded

1 tablespoon tamarind paste

50ml hot water

2 small Thai shallots, chopped

2 garlic cloves, peeled

1 lemongrass stalk, peeled and chopped

1 thumb-sized piece of galangal, chopped

1 thumb-sized piece of fresh root ginger, peeled and chopped

50ml vegetable oil

1 teaspoon chilli powder

¼ fresh pineapple, peeled, cored and roughly chopped

200g crunchy peanut butter

20g palm sugar

salt, to taste

*Until recently, I have typically cooked the Thai-style satay or sate, but since my visit to Malaysia and a trip to a satay stall in Malacca, I have been swayed and now love these with their sauce sweetened with pineapple. So proud are the Malays of their satay that you are even served them as a little treat on the national airline and they are good. Yes, airline food that is good. Note, beware of your white shirt, as the sauce can properly stain your clothes. You can of course buy a jar of satay sauce, but this one is worth the effort.*

Heat a small, dry frying pan until hot, then add the ground spices and toast until fragrant, shaking the pan regularly. Remove from the heat.

Put the rest of the ingredients, except the pork, into a food processor and blend to a paste, then add the toasted spices and blend to mix. In a bowl, rub this mixture all over the pork to coat, then cover and leave to marinate for at least 2 hours.

When you are nearly ready to cook, soak 20 wooden skewers in cold water for 20 minutes, then drain – this prevents them from burning during cooking.

Meanwhile, make your satay sauce. Soak the dried chillies in hot water for 20 minutes to soften, then drain. Combine the tamarind paste and hot water to make a purée.

Blend the soaked chillies, shallots, garlic, lemongrass, galangal and ginger in a food processor (or in a bowl using a hand-held blender) to make a smooth paste. Add the vegetable oil and mix well.

Heat a wok over a medium heat until hot, then reduce the heat to low, add the paste and chilli powder and cook slowly for about 10 minutes until fragrant and dark.

Blend the pineapple to a purée and add to the wok, along with the peanut butter, tamarind purée and palm sugar, and bring to the boil over a medium heat. Keep stirring so it doesn't stick. Reduce the heat to low and cook for 10 minutes, or until the sauce has thickened and there is oil on the surface. Season to taste.

Thread the pork pieces onto the soaked wooden skewers. Heat a large griddle pan or BBQ until hot, then add the skewers and cook on each side for 5–7 minutes or until the pork is cooked through.

Serve the hot skewers on a serving plate or board, with the warm satay sauce in a small serving bowl alongside.

The Malaysians love their coconuts and this delivery to Seremban market was enough for just one day's worth of cooking! Here I'm helping grill some pork satays in Malacca, to be served once done with a fresh peanut and pineapple sauce, and I loved these chicken wings, cooked on the street in Chinatown, Kuala Lumpur.

# FERMENTED, RAW & CURED

'Leave it alone' has long been one of the greatest pieces of cookery advice dispensed to me. The objective is to allow nature to show off its finery and for the cook to simply trust in the most basic yet scientific of preparations. And alongside the traditional processes an exciting new world of raw food, curing and fermenting is now opening up, combining techniques from Korea and Japan with the bold flavours of countries like Mexico and Peru.

# MARINATED SCALLOP SALAD, CUCUMBER AND SOY

**ENOUGH FOR 4–6 ON
LITTLE PLATES**

1 cucumber

8 scallops

a handful of fresh
  coriander leaves

1 tablespoon light soy sauce

*For the dressing*

2 small fresh red chillies

4 teaspoons fish sauce

4 teaspoons lime juice

2 teaspoons palm sugar

*Thinly sliced scallops marinated for just a few minutes are soft and delicious, but also very quick and very easy. Don't think that these pretty plates are complicated, on the contrary.*

Cut the cucumber into ribbons using a vegetable peeler.

Pound all the dressing ingredients together in a mortar and pestle.

Slice the scallops horizontally using a very sharp knife and arrange with the cucumber ribbons, coriander and dressing. Dribble the soy over, leave for 2 minutes, then serve.

# VIETNAMESE RICE PAPER ROLLS

**MAKES 12–14 ROLLS**

### For the dressing

4 fresh green chillies,
  2 de-seeded, 2 left whole

6 garlic cloves, peeled

4 fresh coriander roots, soaked
  and washed

large pinch of salt

4 small Thai shallots, halved

60g palm sugar

80ml fresh lime juice

4 teaspoons fish sauce

### For the noodle mix and salad

50g dried rice vermicelli

3 small Thai shallots, sliced

100g carrots, peeled and cut
  into julienne

100g daikon radish, cut
  into julienne

100g spring onions, cut into
  julienne

a big handful of beansprouts

a small bunch of fresh mint,
  leaves picked

a small bunch of fresh Thai
  basil, leaves picked

a small bunch of fresh
  coriander, leaves picked

12–14 rice paper sheets

12–14 choy sum leaves

*There are snacks and treats that we know are good for us, and these ones are not just healthy, they make you feel good when you eat them, too. I have sat and watched many a person make these in various places around the world, both in restaurants and on the streets, and one day I will get to Vietnam and fulfil a dream of having rice paper rolls in Saigon. The rice paper itself is so cool, it is paper thin and, when you know how to use it, it is simple to work with.*

Using a mortar and pestle, pound all the chillies, garlic, coriander roots and salt together, then add the shallots and pound to a paste. Add the palm sugar and pound again to a paste. Mix in the lime juice and fish sauce and taste – it should be really powerful as it is a salad dressing. Set to one side.

Soak the noodles in warm water for about 30 minutes, then drain and cut into 2cm pieces. Add half the dressing and toss together so the noodles take it up.

In a separate bowl, mix all the vegetables and beansprouts together, but not the herbs. Add a little dressing and toss to wilt the veg, then mix in some of each of the herbs.

For the rice paper rolls, I have a bowl of cold water and a large tea towel at the ready. Working with one at a time, I dip each rice paper sheet into the water until it starts to soften (which only takes a few seconds) and then drop the wilted paper onto the tea towel and flatten it by patting the top.

Next, lay the soaked rice paper sheet on a board or the worktop, take a bundle of the dressed salad and lay it on nicely, then lay some of the dressed noodles on top, topped with a choy sum leaf. Now arrange some of the herbs on top so a few stick out over the end. Roll up the paper tightly around the filling, then transfer the roll to a plate or tray.

Repeat with the remaining rice paper sheets, salad, noodles, choy sum leaves and herbs.

Cover the rolls with clingfilm until you are ready to serve. They will sit very happily for a good few hours but must be eaten on the day they are made.

# QUICK KIMCHI WITH PEARS

......................................................................

**MAKES ABOUT 1.2KG**

1 Korean cabbage
(about 1.2kg)

400g salt

60g fresh root ginger, peeled

10 garlic cloves, peeled

8 tablespoons gochugaru
(Korean ground chilli)

6 tablespoons fish sauce

1 nashi (Asian) pear, cored

5 large or 10 small spring
onions, roughly chopped

*(handwritten margin notes: 80, 1z, 2, ½, ½, 2)*

*Kimchi is the most essential food in all of Korea. It is eaten with every meal, including breakfast. It is so important that the Korean government spent a fortune on developing a kimchi that could be eaten in space by their astronauts. This is a quick recipe which you can make at home, but you will need a container that has a tight-fitting lid or your fridge will suffer.*

......................................................................

Slice the cabbage in half and rinse under cold water to remove any dirt, then shake off any excess.

Mix the salt and 2 litres of water together to make your brining solution. Add the cabbage halves, cut side down, and completely submerge them in the water, setting a chopping board (or other heavy object) on top to weigh them down. Set aside for 30–60 minutes (depending on the size of your cabbage) until the leaves have completely softened.

While the cabbage is soaking, make the kimchi paste. Put all the remaining ingredients, except the spring onions, into a blender and whizz together until the mixture forms a purée. Pour the purée into a large bowl, then add the spring onions and mix into a thick paste.

Drain the cabbage halves and rinse thoroughly under cold water to remove the salt. Do this carefully, otherwise the finished kimchi will be too salty. The leaves should be soft and malleable. Squeeze out any water, separate the leaves, then add the cabbage to the bowl to cover with the paste.

To coat the cabbage, take a handful of the kimchi paste and rub it up and down each individual leaf – taking particular care to coat the thicker, inside white parts as these need more seasoning, then use any remaining paste to coat the thinner green leaves.

Transfer to an airtight container and store in the fridge until needed. You can put a layer of clingfilm over the container, under the lid, to double seal it, if you like. Kimchi can be eaten fresh on the day it is made, but the taste intensifies over time. The longer it's left, the tangier it becomes – which in turn makes it better for cooking with. It will keep for up to 12 months in the fridge if stored correctly.

# SEA BASS TATAKI, ENOKI MUSHROOM SALAD

**SERVES 6**

250g sea bass, thinly sliced (the thickness of smoked salmon)

15g dried wakame or 70g fresh wakame

3 spring onions, sliced on an angle

10g pickled ginger, chopped

a handful of fresh coriander leaves

1 cucumber, peeled and cut into julienne

50g enoki mushrooms, wiped and stalk ends trimmed

100g salmon roe or flying fish roe (if possible)

*For the dressing*

3 tablespoons dashi (mixed according to packet instructions)

3 tablespoons dark soy sauce

3 tablespoons tamari

60ml sake

60ml mirin

50g sugar

*When sashimi is beaten until it is very thin and flat it is known as tataki. You can do this with salmon or tuna, but I like to make tataki of sea bass, which feels very extravagant because of the cost of the fish. It is served with a dressing of mirin, dashi, sake and two kinds of soy sauce. The wakame used in the salad is a lobe-leaf seaweed that can be bought salted and dried. It needs to be soaked before use to get rid of the salt and to rehydrate.*

Slice the sea bass downwards into six thin pieces. Create six plate-sized pieces of clingfilm and put them in a row on a solid bench or worktop.

Now lay the sea bass slices in the centre of each clingfilm piece, butting up against each other. The sea bass should only take up a third of the space at the moment as it will be beaten. Take another sheet of clingfilm and lay it over the top, then hammer the fish until it's wafer thin. A rolling pin works well, or a flat metal bat. All the slices of fish will join together as you do so. Start to move out to fill the plate-sized round.

Peel off the top layer of clingfilm, then lift the bottom layer and flip over carefully on to serving plates, so that the fish is transferred without tearing. Peel off the layer of clingfilm that is now on top.

If the wakame seaweed is dried, soak in warm water for 20 minutes, rinse and squeeze dry. Mix the dried or fresh seaweed with the spring onions, pickled ginger, coriander leaves, cucumber and enoki mushrooms.

Make a dressing with the dashi, dark soy sauce, tamari, sake and mirin and sweeten with the sugar. Mix half the dressing with the wakame salad and leave to sit for 5 minutes.

Pour a tablespoon or so of the remaining dressing over each plate of fish. Pile the salad in the centre and garnish with a good teaspoon of salmon eggs.

# 머리조심
## Head careful

The Koreans love fermented foods, from kimchi to spicy pastes called jang, traditionally fermented in these huge pots. Eat alongside other fantastic ingredients such as the freshest bean sprouts in the world or fried chicken – a national obsession!

# SZECHUAN SPICED BEEF

......................................................

FOR 2

*For the beef*

1 teaspoon white peppercorns

2 teaspoons Szechuan
  peppercorns

1 teaspoon coriander seeds

200g beef fillet

50ml olive oil

1 teaspoon sea salt


*For the kohlrabi salad*

2 teaspoons wasabi

a handful of fresh flat-leaf
  parsley, chopped

30g capers, chopped

100g Japanese mayonnaise

250g kohlrabi, cut into julienne

juice of 1 small lime

salt and freshly ground
  black pepper


olive oil, to drizzle

lime wedges, to serve

*These little Szechuan peppercorns are very powerful and as youngsters
we called them gunpowder. The sensation is a tingling one and they fill
the mouth with the most wonderful flavour, but they must be cooked, so
sear the beef really well over a very high heat.*

......................................................

Toast the peppercorns and coriander seeds, then lightly crush.

Trim the beef fillet and rub with the olive oil, salt and crushed spices.
Wrap the fillet in clingfilm tightly and leave to marinate overnight.

Sear the fillet for 3–5 minutes in a hot griddle pan or over a BBQ until
sealed on all sides, then cool.

Add the wasabi, parsley and capers to the mayonnaise and adjust the
seasoning. Mix the kohlrabi with some salt and lime and leave for
5 minutes, then dress with the mayonnaise.

Slice the beef very thinly and arrange in a single layer on a plate.

Arrange the kohlrabi salad on the plate, drizzle with olive oil and serve
with lime wedges.

# LIME-CURED SQUID, FENNEL AND MUSTARD GREENS

**ENOUGH FOR 6**

1 large squid tube, cleaned

1 small fennel bulb, leaves removed

30ml extra virgin olive oil

juice of 2 limes

3 mustard green leaves, shredded

a handful of fresh flat-leaf parsley leaves, chopped

1 small fresh red chilli, cut into julienne

salt and freshly ground black pepper

*The squid is just cooked in this recipe with the smallest amount of heat, and I mean the smallest. The lime is strong and powerful, so the portion size should be small. This is a taster plate and in no way a meal.*

To prepare the squid, open the cleaned squid tube from top to bottom and lay out flat on a chopping board. Using a sharp knife, slice into the thinnest of long strips and set to one side.

Slice the fennel leaves as thinly as possible on a mandolin. Mix the shaved fennel with a large pinch of salt and leave to cure.

Now for the squid. Heat a frying pan and get it really hot. Mix the squid with a little olive oil. Mix the lime juice and remaining olive oil with a little salt in a large mixing bowl.

Drop the squid into the pan and give it a shuffle for 30 seconds and that's it.

Put the squid in the lime and olive oil mix, drop the fennel on top and mix. Now add the rest of the ingredients and leave to sit and cure properly for 5 minutes before serving.

# MARINATED SEA TROUT IN PICKLED DAIKON

**MAKES 4–6 LITTLE PLATES**

*For the pickled daikon*

500ml Japanese rice vinegar

75g sugar

50ml mirin

½ daikon radish, peeled and
   thinly sliced into rounds

*For the sea trout*

2 tablespoons Japanese
   rice vinegar

30ml light soy sauce

300g sea trout, chopped

6 fresh chives, chopped

*To serve*

pickled ginger

wasabi

*Sea trout is a seasonal fish, I am pleased to say, and therefore only available at certain times of the year. This salad is all about Australia, where sea trout are fished in the Tasman Sea. Use sea trout sparingly – it's very delicate and not at all strong like salmon nor bony like trout. You need to make the pickle in advance as it takes an hour, but it will then keep for weeks.*

To make the pickle, bring the vinegar, sugar and mirin to the boil, then set aside to cool. Pour the vinegar mix over the sliced daikon and allow to steep for 1 hour.

For the sea trout, mix the vinegar and the soy together. Mix the sea trout with the dressing.

Serve on little plates with a spoon of the sea trout over slices of pickled radish. Sprinkle over the chives and arrange some pickled ginger and fresh wasabi on the side.

# CHOPPED SALMON AND KIMCHI TACOS

**SERVES 4–6**

*For the pickled red onions*

100ml rice, coconut or
  apple vinegar

100g caster sugar

1 red onion, finely sliced

*For the salmon*

4 teaspoons vegetable oil

100ml lime juice

3 drops of good-quality
  sesame oil

25ml olive oil

100ml coconut vinegar

4 teaspoons fish sauce

4 teaspoons sugar syrup

200g skinless salmon fillet, very
  finely diced

*To serve*

½ cucumber, half peeled, de-
  seeded and diced

2 spring onions, very
  finely sliced

a handful of fresh coriander,
  roughly chopped

kimchi (bought or see
  page 244)

stack of small soft white corn
  taco shells

100g Japanese mayonnaise

*As I travel, the more I am seeing the new and the old worlds coming together with wonderful culinary creations. The youth of Seoul have decided on a new tack altogether; they are taking not just one, but sometimes three, cultures and bringing them together. This is the type of street food that is being born out of that, combining their love of kimchi – it is served with every meal, and I mean every meal – and a desire to introduce new foods to the young and not-so-young people of South Korea's capital.*

For the pickled red onions, put the vinegar and sugar into a pot and bring to the boil. Remove from the heat as soon as it comes to the boil, leave to cool for 2 minutes, then drop in the onion and stir. Set to one side until cold.

For the salmon, mix all the liquids together in a bowl, then add the salmon, stir, and leave for 10 minutes.

To assemble and serve, mix together the cucumber, spring onions, coriander and pickled red onion slices and add to the salmon mixture. Stir well.

Warm the taco shells according to the packet instructions.

Spoon the salmon mixture and kimchi into the tacos, then squidge some Japanese mayo over each one. Serve immediately.

*Step-by-step pictures on pages 256–257*

# RAW TUNA SALAD WITH SOBA NOODLES

FOR 4

200g soba noodles

300g A-grade tuna belly, sliced

2 sheets of toasted nori

2 small spring onions, cut at
an angle

50g wasabi

*For the dipping sauce*

350ml dashi (mixed according
to packet instructions)

50ml soy sauce

20ml mirin

20g sugar

*Soba noodles are traditionally eaten cold and combined with a dipping sauce of soy and dashi, as here. The method for cooking the soba noodles was taught to me by a Japanese lady 20 years ago and it works wonderfully. Buy the best soba noodles you can and enjoy.*

First make the dipping sauce. Combine the dashi, the soy, half the mirin and the sugar in a saucepan and heat until the sugar dissolves. Do not boil. Cool and add the remaining mirin to the pan.

Fill a saucepan three-quarters full of cold water and bring to the boil. Salt well. Add the noodles, separating them as they go in. Allow the water to return to the boil, then remove the noodles with a strainer and quickly shock them in a bowl of ice-cold water. Repeat this process twice more. Drain the noodles. Lay out on a tray and chill in the fridge.

Drop the noodles into the dipping sauce, then take out of the sauce and place on a plate with the raw tuna. Crumble and sprinkle over the toasted nori and serve with the spring onions, wasabi and the dipping sauce on the side.

# PRAWN TARTARE WITH BEANSPROUT FRITTERS

**ENOUGH FOR 6 AS A
LITTLE TASTER**

*For the prawn tartare*

200g peeled school prawns or
    small sweet prawns

50ml lime juice

pinch of salt

a small handful of fresh flat-leaf
    parsley, finely chopped

*For the beansprout fritters*

100g plain flour

20g cornflour

1 teaspoon salt

½ teaspoon white pepper

1 teaspoon baking powder

2 long fresh red chillies,
    finely diced

100ml vegetable oil, for frying

200g beansprouts

fresh coriander leaves,
    to garnish

*Little school prawns are best for this dish – the smaller and sweeter the
better. This recipe is not in any way difficult, but the result is very special.
It seems that we in the West are the only people who treat beansprouts
as a salad item. In the East they are usually cooked or put through a hot
dish, but regardless, they are always cleaned in the same way as we clean
a bean – topped and tailed.*

Make the batter for the fritters in the usual way by mixing the flours, salt,
pepper and baking powder together.

Add 150ml water and mix to a smooth batter, then drop in the chilli.

Heat the oil in a large frying pan.

Wash and drain the beansprouts well, then mix them gently into the
batter. Take little spoonfuls and drop into the heated oil. Leave to cook
for 2 minutes, then flip over and leave to cook for a further 2 minutes –
they should be crispy on the outside and squidgy in the middle. Take out
and place on kitchen paper to drain the oil off.

Chop the prawns roughly and mix with the lime juice, salt and parsley,
and serve immediately with the fritters, sprinkled with coriander.

# STAR ANISE-CURED SALMON WITH A SHALLOT DRESSING

**ENOUGH FOR A CROWD**

3 star anise

2 teaspoons black peppercorns

1 tablespoon coriander seeds

1 tablespoon juniper berries

1 tablespoon fennel seeds

5 bay leaves

2 lemongrass stalks

700g brown sugar

500g rock salt

a few sprigs of fresh thyme

1.5kg salmon fillet, skin on

1 tablespoon vegetable oil

*For the dressing*

2 small banana shallots,
   finely diced

1 tablespoon red wine vinegar

1 tablespoon olive oil

*This is a cured recipe whose inspiration came from gravlax. As much as I love the flavour of dill, it never really sits well on a menu alongside lots of Asian dishes, so after much experimenting we came up with this. It's sweet and salty and has that wonderful flavour of Southeast Asia. The salmon can be cured overnight, but it actually only needs a few hours to be successful.*

Blend the spices, bay leaves and lemongrass in a blender or mortar and pestle, then mix with the sugar, salt and thyme.

Sprinkle some of the salt and sugar mix over a large tray, then put the salmon on top and pack the rest of the sugar and salt over to form a crust. Leave at room temperature for at least 6 hours or for 12–24 hours in the fridge, turning occasionally.

To make the dressing, marinate the shallots in the red wine vinegar while you prepare the salmon, then blend with the olive oil.

When the salmon has finished marinating, wipe off the salt and sugar mix and dry well. Rub the salmon with the vegetable oil and quickly sear on both sides in a griddle pan.

Allow to rest, then cut into thin slices. Lay the salmon on a plate and serve the dressing on the side.

*Step-by-step pictures on pages 262–263*

# RAW TUNA, CUCUMBER AND HERBS WITH SOY AND CHILLI

......................................................

**ENOUGH FOR 4–6 ON LITTLE PLATES**

50g glass noodles (mung bean thread or cellophane noodles)

1 small cucumber

200g A-grade tuna, cut into 5mm dice

a small handful of fresh coriander

a small handful of fresh Thai basil

*For the dressing*

juice and zest of 1 lime

1 fresh green chilli, finely diced

1 fresh red chilli, finely diced

100ml Chinese (Shaoxing) rice wine

50ml mirin

25ml dark soy

25ml rice vinegar

*Tuna tartare is a classic and always will be because it is simply ace. You can be as fancy as you like, but served with just a few crispy bits like the Fried Garnish on page 204, fried plantain or corn chips, it is also a joy.*

......................................................

Soak the glass noodles in boiling water for 2 minutes until hydrated, then drain. Cut the cucumber into ribbons using a vegetable peeler.

Make the dressing by mixing all the ingredients together.

Mix the dressing with the noodles and the cucumber and leave to soak for 10 minutes, until the noodles take up lots of the dressing. Drain off the excess and put into a small bowl.

Mix a good tablespoon of the dressing with the tuna and leave to sit.

Mix the herbs with the noodles and cucumber. Arrange on little plates and serve with extra dressing on the side.

# Index

apples: apple and granola crumble with labneh 19
    honey and apple tea cake 24
aubergines: miso baked aubergine with brown rice salad 92
    peppered tofu with aubergine 102
Aussie-style grains bowl 38
avocados: removing seed 16
    avocado and prawn tempura 54
    avocado, chorizo and spinach with cream dressing
    on rye 16

bacon: kimchi fried rice with pork and egg 190
bamboo shoots: pork red curry with bamboo 136
banh pho: phat Thai 208
basil salad with fennel, coriander and chilli 94
bean curd: pork and bean curd rolls 56–7
    *see also* tofu
beans *see* green beans; mung beans; snake beans
beansprouts: bibimbap 194–5
    lamb salad with beansprouts and chilli 96
    prawn tartare with beansprout fritters 259
beef: beef rendang 152
    bibimbap 194–5
    chilled Korean noodles 202
    Szechuan spiced beef 248
    Vietnamese grilled beef with glass noodle salad 212
bibimbap 194–5
bindaettoek 49
blackberries: honey and apple tea cake with blackberry
    crème fraîche 24
blueberry and coconut pancakes 18
bossam 66
bream: jungle curry of fish 156
    whole bream, pomelo and herb salad 232
butternut squash: butternut squash red curry with tofu 144
    pumpkin noodles with lime pickle 198
    sour yellow curry of vegetables 154
    spicy prawns and scallops with pumpkin 139

cabbage: quick kimchi with pears 244
carrots: bibimbap 194–5
    Vietnamese rice paper rolls 242
celeriac: pigeon, celeriac purée and Szechuan
    gunpowder 130
char kway teow 186
Chiang Mai noodles with chicken 188
chicken: Chiang Mai noodles with chicken 188
    congee with chicken and chilli oil 30
    crab, chicken and glass noodle salad 70
    curry puffs 68
    grilled coconut chicken and peanut salad 84
    Korean chicken filled with rice 193
    Korean Fried Chicken 114
    ma hor 64
    massaman chicken and prawn curry 158
    satay chicken noodles 192

spiced crab with glass noodles 81
spicy chicken stew 127
Thai green chicken curry 146
tom kha gai 164
whole spatchcocked chicken with lemon and herbs 220
chilled Korean noodles 202
chillies: roasting 184
    bibimbap 194–5
    fried garnish 204
    green beans, chilli and sesame seeds 106
    green papaya salad 50
    hot shallot and lemongrass sambal 80
    la la chilli and fat noodles 200
    lamb salad with beansprouts and chilli 96
    langoustines in chilli jam 214
    Malaysian rice and sambal 206
    raw tuna, cucumber and herbs with soy and chilli 264
    roasted chilli powder 70
    roasted chilli powder 70
    sticky chilli sauce 114
    sweet basil salad with fennel, coriander and chilli 94
    sweet chilli sauce 47
    XO sauce 126
    *see also* curries
Chinese duck noodle soup 172
choo chee fish 141
chorizo: avocado, chorizo and spinach with cream dressing
    on rye 16
cinnamon and nashi pear French toast 20
clams: la la chilli and fat noodles 200
coconut milk: beef rendang 152
    butternut squash red curry with tofu 144
    Chiang Mai noodles with chicken 188
    choo chee fish 141
    coconut rice 163
    grilled coconut chicken and peanut salad 84
    massaman chicken and prawn curry 158
    pear and okra with coconut dressing 86
    pork red curry with bamboo 136
    roti jala 153
    spicy prawns and scallops with pumpkin 139
    Thai green chicken curry 146
    tom kha gai 164
coconut milk yoghurt: blueberry and coconut pancakes 18
cod: choo chee fish 141
    cod with miso and green bean salad 224
    Thai fish cakes 44
combination soup 168
congee with chicken and chilli oil 30
courgettes: bibimbap 194–5
crab: crab, chicken and glass noodle salad 70
    spiced crab with glass noodles 81
cucumbers: Malay mixed salad 80
    marinated scallop salad, cucumber and soy 240
    raw tuna, cucumber and herbs with soy and chilli 264
curries: beef rendang 152
    butternut squash red curry with tofu 144
    choo chee fish 141

First published in 2018 by HEADLINE HOME
An imprint of HEADLINE PUBLISHING GROUP

1

Cataloguing in Publication Data is available from the British Library

Hardback ISBN 978 1 4722 25863

eISBN 978 1 4722 26662

Commissioning editor: Muna Reyal

Designed by Mark Harper at Bonbon London

Photography: Yuki Sugiura

Food styling: Lizzie Kamenetzky

Food styling assistant: Katie Marshall

Art director and prop styling: Cynthia Inions

Editor: Kay Halsey-Delves

Project editor: Kate Miles

Proofreaders: Annie Lee and Miren Lopategui

Indexer: Caroline Wilding

Repro at BORN Group

Printed and bound in China through Great Wall Printing Co. Ltd.

HEADLINE PUBLISHING GROUP
An Hachette UK Company
Carmelite House
50 Victoria Embankment
London EC4Y 0DZ

www.headline.co.uk
www.hachette.co.uk

# ACKNOWLEDGEMENTS

There would be no me and therefore no book without inspiration and guidance. My journey started many years ago and along the way I have met, chatted and cooked with the most amazing people. To anyone who has ever shown me something in the world of food, thank you, you are the reason I can write this book and cook the way I do.

To the gochu-gang, you have made this book a joy to work on. Every one of you knows how much I admire your individual talents and inspiration. You have made it easy to cook and tell stories, drink tea and bring this book to life. Lizzie Kamenetzky and Katie Marshall, all that shopping and cooking and washing up and the smiles – you two are ace. Cynthia Inions, for always making me laugh and adding that special bit of sparkling Cynthia dust to every page. The ever incredible Yuki Sugiura for your most wonderful patience and beautiful photography – no one does it better. Mark Harper, you know how special you are to me, I love your designs and always will – to the future. Kay Halsey-Delves, my editor, thank you for taking the time to guide me through troubled waters – your patience in deciphering my scribble is not forgotten. To Muna Reyal, for believing and always being around when the conversations needed to be had. And to Kate Miles, for all the positive words along the way.

Jo Carlton and Jonathan Conway, thank you both.

To Grace Kitto, Dan Chambers, Amanda Ross, Sally Quick and Kate Norum, the Good Food Channel, Janice Gabriel, my Korean crew and every director, camera and sound person I have travelled with over the years – the drivers, the fixers, the shopkeepers and stallholders. I have loved every adventure.

Lastly, to a girl who believes in me and has pushed me to put into print what I really believe and love. Thank you Lisa.

That's it from me for a little while. If you feel I have missed you out, I'm sorry, please let me know.

I am off now on my next adventure…

John Torode is one of the UK's best-loved chefs and judge of BBC One's *MasterChef, Celebrity MasterChef* and *Junior MasterChef.* John's food and travel series, *Australia, Malaysian Adventures, Korean Food Tour* and *John Torode's Asia* have aired on the Good Food Channel.